AF472542

Dr. Bohannon presents a clear picture of the original organizational structure of the church of Christ, relying on extensive research centered on the biblical record and effectively making the case for the development of a local church planning process to "help a congregation to grow, to solve problems and to make decisions that everyone understands and that everyone has bought into and supports." This scholarly work also makes the case for the involvement and participation of every member in the work of the church and its basic mission of teaching the gospel of Christ. It is a resource for church leaders, teachers and members who want to restore the true pattern of the church and enrich their Christian service.

— Don McKee, Bible teacher, author, columnist for the Marietta Daily Journal, former Associated Press staff writer and bureau chief of U.S. News & World Report.

The Organization and Leadership of the First Century Church: A Study

Dr. Richard R. Bohannon

Copyright © 2011 Dr. Richard R. Bohannon

All rights reserved. No part of this book may be used or reproduced by any means, graphic, electronic, or mechanical, including photocopying, recording, taping or by any information storage retrieval system without the written permission of the publisher except in the case of brief quotations embodied in critical articles and reviews.

WestBow Press books may be ordered through booksellers or by contacting:

WestBow Press
A Division of Thomas Nelson
1663 Liberty Drive
Bloomington, IN 47403
www.westbowpress.com
1-(866) 928-1240

Because of the dynamic nature of the Internet, any web addresses or links contained in this book may have changed since publication and may no longer be valid. The views expressed in this work are solely those of the author and do not necessarily reflect the views of the publisher, and the publisher hereby disclaims any responsibility for them.

Any people depicted in stock imagery provided by Thinkstock are models, and such images are being used for illustrative purposes only.

Certain stock imagery © Thinkstock.

ISBN: 978-1-4497-1342-3 (sc)
ISBN: 978-1-4497-1343-0 (dj)
ISBN: 978-1-4497-1341-6 (e)

Library of Congress Control Number: 2011924138

A Reader's Guide to the Holy Bible: King James Version. (1972). Camden, NJ: Thomas Nelson Inc.

The Open Bible: New King James Version. (1997). Nashville, TN: Thomas Nelson Publishers.

Printed in the United States of America

WestBow Press rev. date: 3/18/2011

To my wife, Sandra, who has patiently listened to all my arguments, constructs, and lessons taught around the contents of this manuscript; to my daughter, Sonua, and to my son, Rick, his wife, Anna, and my granddaughter, Sylva.

Also, to the many who have encouraged me in my writing of this book, especially, Don McKee, the patient reader, editor, and encourager.

To every Christian who desires to worship in spirit and in truth as Christians did in the first century church.

"Be diligent to present yourself approved to God, a worker who does not need to be ashamed, rightly dividing the word of truth." II Timothy 2:15

Contents

Introduction

The Study

Have you considered what the organization and leadership of the church of Christ looked like during the first century of Christianity? It is problematic to me that one may have much difficulty finding the church of Christ that is presented in God's Word and so this study began with that problem in mind.

The purpose of this study was to read, examine, and offer meaning to the New Testament church of Christ within the framework of organization development. This study has a dual purpose: 1) to examine the Scriptures and describe the organism (structure) and the organization of the first century church; and 2) to examine the Scriptures and describe the leadership of the first century church of Christ. The hypothesis is that the organization and leadership of the church, as Jesus intended it to be and instructed the early church leaders, is not what we see practiced in the various Christian religious groups today. The scriptural church of Christ has been institutionalized to a great extent, both in structure and in understanding.

This study utilized a qualitative research methodology utilizing content analysis as its design. Leedy and Ormrod (2005) define content analysis as "a detailed and systematic examination of the contents of a particular body of material for the purpose of identifying patterns, themes, or biases" (p. 142). Translations of early secular writings about the first century church were examined but the principle body of material that was used to examine the organization and leadership of the church of Christ was the Bible, God's Holy Scriptures. *The Open Bible New King James Version*

(1997) translation was the primary translation used but occasional use of other translations was necessary for comparison purposes.

The themes and patterns that emerged from this study do not reflect the hundreds of Christian church groups (http://religions.pewforum.org) that one observes in today's world and so begs the question of whether Christians ought to begin again to look to God's Word for their foundation and look to return to the church of Christ as depicted in the original Word. It will be left up to the individual reader to compare these findings with his or her particular Christian worship group and determine whether there are differences between a particular Christian group and the church of Christ as described in the New Testament. This is recommended because there are literally hundreds of Christian religious groups and it is well beyond the scope of this study to make comparisons of the various groups that fall under the Christian umbrella.

The content of the Scriptures was systematically examined for the purpose of identifying patterns and themes that specifically dealt with the organization of the church of Christ and the scriptural leadership model of the church of Christ. A very important point in this study is that the Scriptures were viewed as being eternal in accordance with Psalm 119:160, Isaiah 40:8, and I Peter 1:25. There have been numerous doctrines or interpretations written by men in numerous Christian religious groups to supersede, and in some cases, replace the Scriptures. These man-made documents appear to be part of the problem of why the organization and leadership of the church of Christ today looks so different than that presented in the Scriptures. This writing is not intended to replace, supersede, or interpret God's Word—it is intended to provide an emphasis to encourage those of the Christian faith to examine the Bible as the true source of God's Word as it relates to the structure of the church and its leadership model.

Another important point of this study is how the church of the Lord is defined. The word *church* is derived from the Greek word *ekklesia* and it simply means an assembly or gathering. I offer a different yet scriptural definition of church—and that definition is "a body of believers who are called out into a unified, loving, and covenant relationship with Jesus and with each other."

People often say, "We are going to church" when in fact they mean and should say, "We are going to worship." The building that one is going to is not the church but many look at the Old Testament tabernacle and temple and the many historical religious buildings that have been built and think a building should be built to honor Jesus or God or other religious figures. Our favorite apostle and disciple, outspoken Peter, proposed the construction of three temples during the transfiguration (Matthew 17:1-13; Mark 9:2-13; Luke 9:28-36), but the apostles later came to realize that the Christian disciples or followers of Jesus were and are the building, the church of Christ (I Corinthians 3:9). Buildings, when used in the first century, were simply utilized as an expedient place to meet and carry out the mission of the church during that time. Other misuses of the word *church* are when it is used to denote a denomination or when it is used to identify a single organized religious group. The use of the word *church* in the Scriptures refers to the universal church of Christ or to any of its autonomous congregations of the Lord.

There are some limitations that came into play for this study. It is limited in that it is through the lens of organization development and is not a historical or theological study but nonetheless conducted by a convicted Christian. I am well aware that I am neither a Bible historian nor an authority on Christian theology but simply exploring the premise that the Scriptures are "profitable for doctrine" (II Timothy 3:16-17). That it is the only doctrine intended to be used in the church by the founder, Jesus Christ. I believe the Scriptures to be the inspired Word of God and that the Scriptures were not given for private interpretation. After all, Paul advised the Philippians to "work out your own salvation with fear and trembling" (Philippians 2:12) and so we should all do this, albeit in the context of the New Testament Scriptures while keeping in mind that Jesus established one body or church (Ephesians 4:4) and the doctrine for that church is the Scriptures (II Timothy 3:16-17). The study is also limited in that it primarily examined the scriptural organization and leadership of the church of Christ as described in the New Testament; however, the Old Testament was examined for prophecies of the church and its builder or leader. Other post-apostolic writings were examined when they were found to deal with the church's leadership and organization in the first century.

Since organizations are guided by the vision and mission of the founder and that vision and mission become integral in the doctrine and culture of the organization, every person claiming membership in the organization should want to adhere to the founder's original instruction as long as the founder is in place. That founder, Jesus, is still the head of the church (Colossians 1:18). Jesus told his apostles that he had all authority (Matthew 28:18). He taught them to go and make disciples, baptize them, and teach whoever they baptized to observe all things that he had commanded them

(Mathew 28:18-20). So, quite simplistically, everything Jesus taught his apostles and disciples has been brought down to the present day in only one document, the Bible. It is the only substantial body of literature (doctrine or instructions) that has been left by the founder, head, and eternal leader of the church of Christ.

The noted church historian, F. F. Bruce (1971), found a few references to Christ or Christians in early Roman literature in the form of what he says we would today refer to as police reports: rioting in Rome by Christians (A.D. 49) in the writings of Suetonius (c A.D. 120); Nero tried to blame Christians for the Great Fire of Rome as recorded by Tacitus in his *Romans Annals* (c A.D. 115 -117); and, Pliny, as proconsul of Bithynia, wrote in a report to Emperor Trajan about the advance of Christianity in his province (c A.D. 112).

In Jewish writings during the Tannaitic Period (c. A.D. 70 – 200) there are references to Christ as a "transgressor in Israel, who practiced magic, scorned the words of the wise, led the people astray, and said he had come neither to take away from the law of Moses nor to add to it (or according to another reading, not to take away from the law of Moses but to add to it). … Two earlier Jewish references to him appear in the manuscript tradition of the *Antiquities* of Josephus (composed c. A.D. 93)" (as cited in Bruce, 1971, pp. 165-166). Basically, by far the major body of literature we have today about Jesus is the Scriptures and that is why it was the foundational, historical document examined in this study. According to Lightfoot (2003), by the third of fourth century "… the New Testament books as they are known today constituted the supreme authority for the primitive church" (p. 161). There are other documents that discuss and describe the church in the early years and they will be discussed in this writing at the appropriate places.

This study of the first century church and its leadership and organization, through the lens of organizational development, used the Scriptures (primarily the New Testament) as the historical document that was examined to see what the actual organization of this early church was and what was its leadership structure. Organizational development typically deals with a "planned change process" where leaders of organizations manage the needed change but consider the technical and human aspects of the organization (Schein, 1992, p. 316). However, the "history on the organization's growth and development is not necessarily a good guide to what will succeed in the future because the environment may have changed and, more importantly, internal changes may have altered its unique strengths and weaknesses" (Schein, 1992, p. 314). I posit that over the centuries man has changed or transformed the organization of the scriptural church of Christ as well as the leadership structure of the scriptural church of Christ when it was not needed nor intended to be changed by its founder. These changes have shifted the church away from its earlier strengths as well as its early doctrine or writings. Change might have been necessary and good in some ministries and how those ministries are carried out as the social environment or civilization has advanced, but the basic doctrine has not changed. Changes that have been very beneficial to the church of Christ are the use of the printing press and the use of radio, television, and other media to evangelize unbelievers. From the study, I conclude that present day Christians should espouse the Word of Christ as given in the New Testament as the guiding document in church organization and church leadership. I also conclude that if the Scriptures have not been changed by the founder, then the doctrine, the organization of the church, and the leadership of the church should not have changed!

Why do I say the doctrine, the organization of the church, and the leadership of the church should not have changed? Look at the greatness of the advances made by the early Christians as recorded in the book of Acts: "about three thousand souls were added" to the church (Acts 2:41); "the lord added to the church daily those that were being saved" (Acts 2:47); and "many of them who heard the word believed; and the number of men came to be about five thousand" (Acts 4:4). Can you imagine anything wrong with an organization that is fulfilling its mission at that rate? What happened? The leadership began to move away from the original leadership pattern that it had been given. Leadership in the congregations of the Lord began to be more influenced by the world than it was influencing to the world. It became an institution instead of the body or organism as described in the Scriptures (I Corinthians 12). By the end of the first century the church was becoming institutionalized and its emphasis was becoming internally focused instead of externally focused toward unbelievers and sharing the gospel with them.

James Moffatt (1938), Washburn Professor of Church History at Union Theological Seminary, gives us insight to what was occurring in the church leadership during its infancy. Toward the end of the first century of the existence of the church, a "mono-episcopate" [head elder] began to emerge out of the presbyters [eldership]. Moffatt found no clear reason for this phenomenon which started in Syria and Asia Minor. As this leadership model developed, the church's organizational structure came to be a bishop over the congregation or collection of congregations, the eldership moved to the second tier of leadership, and deacons or assistants became the third tier of congregational ministry. This practice was not common during the time of Ignatius and there were no such leadership structures in Philippi, Corinth, or Rome until later (pp. 44 - 45).

Moffatt (1938) also describes the worship service as primitive during the early years of the first century. These services were conducted "… on the inherited lines of the synagogue, with lessons from the Word [Old Testament Scriptures], prayer and responsive Amens, and a tide of praise which was partly recitation of the psalms antiphonally, partly improvised in the surging devotion of the faithful to their risen Lord" (p. 44). As they became available, New Testament Scriptures and other church related materials were read during these primitive worship services (Ferguson, 1999). If this primitive worship service was acceptable then and caused the church to grow in such numbers, might it not be an appropriate format for today's worship services? During the first century, Moffatt also found that there were only two "sacraments" that were observed by the church of Christ—baptism and the Lord's Supper. We'll discuss these again and in more detail throughout this study.

This study will inform those who are attempting to follow the teachings of Christ, those attempting to become leaders in a Christian congregation, and those who want to be organized in the pattern of the New Testament church of Christ. This study will begin with a couple of chapters about the church—chapter one will be a look at some of those prophesies in the Old Testament of the church and then in chapter two the evidence of how the church came into being as described in the New Testament. I include these scriptural findings in these two chapters because many folks that I have talked to and interviewed about the church do not understand what the church of Christ is as described in the Scriptures. I want folks to have a very clear understanding of the evidence in the Scriptures of the church that Christ came to the earth to establish before presenting the findings about the church of Christ's organization and leadership.

Chapter three will present the organism and the organization of the church of Christ from the Scriptures. The church of Christ is unique in that it is an organism and it is an organization, but many of us today do not make this scriptural distinction between the two. Soon after the church of Christ was established man began to change it and bring into it his perceptions of worldly organizational structure and began to forget about the organism as it is described in I Corinthians 12:12-27 and other passages of Scripture. Towards the end of the first century man also began to institutionalize the church with hierarchical structures that were not in accordance with the Scriptures.

Chapter four will explore the head of the Church as presented in the Scriptures. In an organizational development analysis, the examination of the organization's leadership is essential to understanding all other aspects of the organization under study.

Every organization needs a vision of where it is and where it wants to be in the future and a mission of what it hopes to accomplish and by whose authority. Chapter five presents the authority, the vision, and the mission that Christ had and still has for the church he established. We will see that Jesus had a mission and that the Holy Spirit has a mission, and present the argument that the mission of every ministry of the church of Christ should be linked to the original mission of the church.

In chapter six we will look at the work of the church as set forth in the New Testament. All organizations have some goals and objectives and reaching those goals and objectives requires that someone do some service or produce some results in order for the organization to fulfill those goals and objectives. There is an ages old argument about "works" and "faith" and I hope to clarify what the Scriptures say for the reader about that topic in this chapter.

Chapter seven will examine the culture of the early church based on the evidences included in the Scriptures. That culture dictated the actions of its early members and followed the culture established by its leader, Jesus Christ, as he taught his followers during his three years of recorded activity here on earth. The culture of an organization does not change unless its leadership changes or leadership desires to change the culture.

In chapters eight through eleven, various aspects of leadership and their effect on the church will be examined strictly from a scriptural perspective. Chapter eight will look at the elders' functional role as the congregation's spiritual leaders. The deacons' functional role as well as other spiritual leaders of the various congregational ministries will be discussed in chapter nine. Chapter ten will review women's roles in the first century church.

Chapter eleven will explore the followership role of the members of the church of Christ from a scriptural perspective. Followership is more than just belonging to an organization; it means a partnership with the leaders of the organization and full support of that leadership with reciprocal support of the followers by their respective leaders. Followership may be the biggest misunderstanding that many of us have about the scriptural Christian.

And then in chapter twelve we will examine what the Scriptures reveal about the servant leadership style that Christ Jesus exhibited and how that leadership style should be the primary leadership style of every member in the church of Christ. Chapter thirteen will conclude the study with some points about a planning process in the church and why it is important for all congregations to have such a planning process in place so that they can grow as more believers are added by God to the church. We will also examine why that planning process is scriptural and provide examples of how that process could be carried out.

Jesus gave a stern warning to those that would lead others to stumble. "But whoever causes one of these little ones who believe in Me to stumble, it would be better for him if a millstone were hung around his neck, and he were thrown into the sea" (Mark 9:42). It is not my intent to cause any to stumble; I simply want those who go by the name Christian to be sure that they know why.

Chapter 1
Prophecy of the Church and Its Fulfillment

"Then speak to him, saying,
'Thus says the LORD of hosts, saying:
"Behold, the Man whose name is the BRANCH!
From His place He shall branch out,
And He shall build the temple of the LORD;
Yes, He shall build the temple of the LORD.
He shall bear the glory,
And shall sit and rule on His throne;
So He shall be a priest on His throne,
And the counsel of peace shall be between them
both"' (Zechariah 6:12-13).

When one scans the Christian landscape in today's world, many variations of the Christian religion are found. These variations are referred to as denominations and according to the World Christian Database (www.worldchristaindatatbase.org) there are over nine thousand of these denominations worldwide with about 635 in the United States. This is very confusing to the non-believer as well as the newly baptized Christian. I find it problematic that there are so many groups or denominations, hence the foundation of this study. I hope that this study will clarify to the reader the scriptural church of Christ and its leadership and organization during the first century of its existence.

There are many external and internal influencers or factors in the organization and leadership of the church of Christ. These factors are change, shifting demographics, immigration, generational differences, and technology to name a few. Change occurs very rapidly in our world, and it is mainly driven by technology and globalization. The demographics of American society are changing, and as the demographics of a society change so does its culture. Our society has new immigrants who do not necessarily assimilate into the existing societal and cultural norms; they retain much of the cultural heritage they knew before coming to the United States. There are generational differences that also influence change. Each generation—the silent majority, baby boomers, Gen X, and Gen Y—is unique. Technology and science are ever changing, and consequently it is difficult for one to stay informed about them. We are inundated with media of all sorts, social networks, the Internet, cell phones, television, radio, and so forth. All of these changes bid for our time and have brought about much stress in our society and subsequently to the church. I observe that these external changes all have some influence on the internal structure and leadership of the church in today's society.

Recent studies indicate shifts in "church" demographics. The Barna Group (www.barnagroup.com) compiled these statistics from its recent 2007 study of various U.S. faith groups:

- 8% of US adults classify themselves as evangelicals.
- 35% of US adults consider themselves as born again, but not evangelical.
- Atheists and agnostics make up 10% of adults nationwide.
- 7% of the US population identifies with a faith other than Christianity.
- 69% of adults believe in God when described as the all-powerful, all-knowing, perfect creator of the universe who rules the world today.
- 8% of people believe that God is the total realization of personal human potential.

The Barna Group also found the following in a 2004 survey on social issues:

- One third of born again adults (33%) say that abortion is a morally acceptable behavior, compared with 45% of all adults, 4% of evangelicals, and 71% of atheists and agnostics.
- 30% of all adults consider having a sexual relationship with someone of the same sex is a morally acceptable behavior.
- 14% of elders [generational term, not church elders], 32% of baby boomers, 41% of baby busters and 40% of mosaics consider having a sexual relationship with someone of the same sex a morally acceptable behavior.

And finally, the Barna Group found these percentages of adults who view certain behavior as morally acceptable in its 2003 study:

- 61% of adults view gambling as a morally acceptable behavior.
- 59% say they enjoy sexual thoughts or fantasies about someone.
- Living with someone of the opposite sex without being married, sometimes called co-habitation is acceptable to 60% of American adults.
- Having a sexual relationship with someone of the opposite sex to whom you are not married is acceptable to 42% of adults.
- 38% think looking at pictures of nudity or explicit sexual behavior is acceptable.
- Using profanity is acceptable to 36% of adults.
- Getting drunk, not just social drinking, is okay with 35% of adults.
- Using drugs not prescribed by a physician is acceptable to 17% of adults.

Another study (Survey, 2008) by the Pew Forum on Religion and Public Life found:

- One in four adults, ages 18 to 29, claim no affiliation with a religious institution.
- The majority of these, just over 50%, describe their religion as "nothing in particular."
- Atheists or agnostics account for 4% of the total population.
- The Roman Catholic Church has lost more members than any faith tradition because of affiliation swapping. Affiliation swapping is defined as moving one's membership from one denomination to another.
- On the protestant side, ranks are swelling in non-denominational churches, while Baptists and Methodists traditions are showing net losses.
- More people are identifying themselves as Buddhist than Muslim, although both populations are less than 1% of the total population in the United States.

These changes in demographics and shifts in social and moral issues as well as our experiences in the world influence our views of the organization and leadership of the church of Christ as depicted in the New Testament. We, as Christians, need to examine and learn from some of the common paradigms that have been formed by our worldly experiences, observations, and education in this time of social and cultural change. By examining our paradigms and contrasting them with Biblical Scriptures we will be able to correct our perspective of the organization and leadership of the church, if needed. As we study, our perspectives and paradigms will shift to become Scripture based and hopefully not be influenced by our worldly experiences in organizations and the leadership of those organizations. We will discuss these perspectives throughout this book.

Older Christians are more apt to hold to the traditional, comfortable leadership model of pastors, elders, shepherds, preachers, and deacons in a hierarchical structure because that organizational structure is what they have seen all their lives in the world at large. Younger Christians are striving to be creative with the biblical model to keep up with the rapidly changing socio-economic structures and cultures within their communities. Both of these groups need to closely examine the Scriptures to arrive at the true definition of church, its leadership, and its organization.

All of these factors and probably some not mentioned are influencing the church to the extent that it has been institutionalized. By this, I mean that Christians have been influenced by their individual worldly pursuits. They have brought leadership and organizational structures, based on their secular experiences, into the church without examining whether these experiences are in accord with the church of Christ as depicted in the Scriptures. Christians are warned of this "drifting away" in Hebrews 2:1. And the institutionalization of the church is described by Paul in Colossians 2:8 when he writes, "Beware lest anyone cheat you through philosophy and empty deceit, according to the traditions of men, according to the basic principles of the world, and not according to Christ." The Bible presents a clear framework for church leadership and that, as well as the organization of the first century church of Christ, is what this study is about. This study is not about leadership styles although we will examine servant leadership as presented in the Scriptures and taught by Jesus to his disciples. This study is about leadership in general in the church. How was it authorized by Jesus? How can we do it better today than we are currently doing?

Some folks say, "Well, I just can't understand the Bible." Bronowski (n.d.) wrote these words that I feel are very appropriate for Christians to read and reflect upon as they undertake to read, study, and understand the Scriptures:

> Many people persuade themselves that they cannot understand mechanical things, or that they have no head for figures. These convictions make us feel enclosed and safe, and of course save us a great deal of trouble. But the reader who has a head for anything at all is pretty sure to have a head for whatever he really wants to put his mind to. (p. 6)

Bronowski was writing about understanding science but I make this same argument to those folks who say they cannot understand the Scriptures or cannot understand religion. You can understand if you only apply a few minutes each day to study. Study with someone who is more knowledgeable of the Scriptures. Pray for understanding; and persist in your study. We have institutionalized the church because of our worldly experiences and observations of organizations in the world. We need to go back to the Scriptures to study and learn what God really intended for us to learn about him and about the church he sent his Son to establish. We have institutionalized the scriptural church of Christ because we are exposed to the leadership and organization models we encounter in the secular world. That is where most Christians spend the bulk of their time. Brunner (1958) described this institutionalization this way: "… the essential being of the *Ecclesia* as a spiritual unity, a communion of persons, has in the process been wrought into something else—an institution" (p. 83).

When Christians do study the Scriptures, their thoughts may be influenced by their worldly paradigms instead of being focused on discerning the truth of God's inspired Word. Christians need to study the Bible, God's Word, but they need to do so in an unbiased manner leaving the influence of the world outside their study. Look at the example the Ethiopian eunuch set for us when he replied to Phillip's question, "Do you understand what you are reading?"

To this the eunuch replied, "How can I, unless someone guides me" (Acts 8:26-39). The eunuch did not have the advantage we enjoy. He did not have the complete Bible; he only had a portion of it. So we, too, need to look for guidance and we can find it in honest men of God, through prayer, and through diligent study of the Word. And remember, the last source of God's Word is in the Bible, not some person. We, as Christians, need to spend more time reading and studying God's Scriptures and focus on God's Word when we are functioning in the world. Remember what Luke wrote about the Bereans. "Then the brethren immediately sent Paul and Silas away by night to Berea. When they arrived, they went into the synagogue of the Jews. These were more fair-minded than those in Thessalonica, in that they received the word with all readiness, and searched the Scriptures daily *to find out* whether these things were so" (Acts 17:10-11). These Bereans set the example or benchmark for Christians then and for Christians today.

As we begin this study of the organization of the church and the leadership roles in the church, we need to first examine and understand some of the prophesies of the Old Testament leading up to the establishment of the church of Christ in the New Testament and then how the church of Christ came to be. We will not have space to examine all the Old Testament prophecies concerning the church. Although the doctrine of the church of Christ is recorded in the New Testament, we need to examine the Old Testament prophesies because, as the apostle Paul tells us, "Whatever was written before time was for our learning" (Romans 15:4). Keep in mind as you read and study, that if you can recognize the first century church in the Scriptures, you should also be able to recognize it in the congregations that you attend and worship with today. Why? Because we find in Ephesians 4:4 that there is only one church or body of the Lord.

If we look at the Bible in its entirety, it is obvious that God had a complete plan in mind when he created the world. I certainly am not privy to that entire plan, only those portions he has revealed to all mankind through the Scriptures. Leaders communicate their plan or vision throughout the organization and God did that through the voices of the prophets in the Old Testament. They told of a coming Savior and that he would establish the church here on earth. God communicates today to the Christian through his Word as recorded in the Scriptures. The Scriptures tell us that "when the fullness of time had come, God sent forth His Son" (Galatians 4:4). Jesus came to establish a new covenant and his church. He was empowered by his Father with all authority to bring about the change. That change was resisted by God's people as all people resist change. Typically, people are comfortable in their present state and do not like to go through the difficult work of change. Jesus picked his leaders and spent three years during his earthly ministry teaching them this new doctrine and conditioning them for the change that was to come in God's people through the establishment of the church of Christ or the Lord's church.

Let me again remind you of what I mean when I write about the church of Christ. The word *church* is derived from the Greek word *ekklesia* and it means an assembly or gathering. The called out. This is generally accepted as the definition of church from a scriptural or Biblical perspective. In the words of Fair (1996), *church* is better understood as "a body of people organized into a somewhat autonomous community of believers in Jesus" (p. 28). There are a couple of other Greek words I feel we need to consider when we define church. The first word is *koinonia* meaning communion that creates a covenant relationship of Christ and the believer and of the believers with one another in a partnership or unity. The second word is *agape* meaning "dearness," "affection," "high regard," or "love." From these three Greek words, *ekklesia, koinonia,* and *agape*, I derive a more comprehensive definition of church than is generally used. That definition is: "A body of believers who are called out into a unified, loving, covenant relationship with Jesus and with each other."

I desire that all Christian groups would use this or a similar scriptural definition that brings in the covenant relationship with Jesus and the love that Christians are to exhibit because there was only one church established by the builder (Ephesians 4:4-6). Yet today we find many Christian churches and many definitions of the church of Christ (http://religions.pewforum.org; www.worldchristaindatatbase.org). A clear understanding of the church, as defined in the Scriptures, would hopefully bring the various Christian religious groups closer to unity and away from the strife that separate some groups. Often this strife exists within groups that reputedly belong to the same religious "order."

With all the foundational study aspects out of the way here and in the introduction, we're now ready to really look at the Scriptures with the purpose of looking at some of those occurrences where the church is prophesied. The prophecies concerning the coming of or establishment of the church of Christ as recorded in the New Testament are found in the Old Testament and in the words of Christ in the accounts of the gospels.

Before the Establishment of the Church

First, we will examine what the Old Testament prophets foretold of the church of Christ. Though this work is only interested in the organization and leadership of the church in the New Testament, it is important to understand something of God's people in the Old Testament, the Law that influenced them, and the prophesies they received from the various prophets.

Early in the Bible, we see family units headed by patriarchs such as Adam, Noah, Abraham, Isaac, and Jacob. This patriarchal age lasted until the time of the judges although the patriarchs had also acted as judges and judged those in their families. An example of a family head or patriarch judging someone is found in Genesis 38:24: "And it came to pass, about three months after, that Judah was told, saying, 'Tamar your daughter-in-law has played the harlot; furthermore she is with child by harlotry.'" So Judah said, 'Bring her out and let her be burned!' "

Later, Moses actually initiated the more formal hierarchical practice of judges to rule over the people at the suggestion of his father-in-law. Moses was overworked trying to do all the judging for the children of Israel, the people were standing in long lines waiting for his judgment on various matters, so Moses' father-in-law suggested a process to make these judgments easier on both Moses and the people. That suggestion, and the appointment of these judges, is recorded in Exodus, chapter 18.

> And so it was, on the next day, that Moses sat to judge the people; and the people stood before Moses from morning until evening. So when Moses' father-in-law saw all that he did for the people, he said, "What is this thing that you are doing for the people? Why do you alone sit, and all the people stand before you from morning until evening?"
>
> And Moses said to his father-in-law, "Because the people come to me to inquire of God. When they have a difficulty, they come to me, and I judge between one and another; and I make known the statutes of God and His laws."
>
> So Moses' father-in-law said to him, "The thing that you do *is* not good. Both you and these people who *are* with you will surely wear yourselves out. For this thing is too much for you; you are not able to perform it by yourself. Listen now to my voice; I will give you counsel, and God will be with you: Stand before God for the people, so that you may bring the difficulties to God. And you shall teach them the statutes and the laws, and show them the way in which they must walk and the work they must do. Moreover you shall select from all the people able men, such as fear God, men of truth, hating covetousness; and place *such* over them *to be* rulers of thousands, rulers of hundreds, rulers of fifty, and rulers of tens. And let them judge the people at all times. Then it will be *that* every great matter they shall bring to you, but every small

> matter they themselves shall judge. So it will be easier for you, for they will bear *the burden* with you. If you do this thing, and God so commands you, then you will be able to endure, and the people will also go to their place in peace."
>
> So Moses heeded the voice of his father-in-law and did all that he had said. And Moses chose able men out of all Israel, and made them heads over the people: rulers of thousands, rulers of hundreds, rulers of fifties, and rulers of tens. And so they judged the people at all times; the hard cases they brought to Moses, but they judged every small case themselves.
>
> Then Moses let his father-in-law depart, and he went his way to his own land. (Exodus 18:13-26)

From that point, Judges ruled the children of Israel until the time of Samuel. People, being human, are never completely satisfied with the status quo, not even God's chosen people. We find that after some time, the elders of Israel came to Samuel and requested that he place kings over them because the nations of the world had kings and the children of Israel wanted to be like other nations of the world. Doesn't this sound like some Christians today? They want to be Christians but they also want to be like the society in which they reside. Samuel gives us this account of how kings over the children of Israel came to be:

> Then all the elders of Israel gathered together and came to Samuel at Ramah, and said to him, "Look, you are old, and your sons do not walk in your ways. Now make us a king to judge us like all the nations."
>
> But the thing displeased Samuel when they said, "Give us a king to judge us." So Samuel prayed to the Lord. And the Lord said to Samuel, "Heed the voice of the people in all that they say to you; for they have not rejected you, but they have rejected me, that I should not rule over them. (I Samuel 8:4-7)

From that time forward kings ruled the chosen people of God, the children of Israel, until Jesus came and established his Kingdom on earth, fulfilling the promise of Genesis 3:15. God sent his son to establish a new covenant and subsequently, the church. The Old Testament prophet Jeremiah was one of the prophets who foretold this event.

> Behold, the days are coming, says the Lord, when I will make a new covenant with the house of Judah—not according to the covenant that I made with their fathers in the day *that* I took them by the hand to lead them out of the land of Egypt. My covenant which they broke, though I was a husband to them, says the Lord. But this *is* the covenant that I will make with the house of Israel after those days, says the Lord: I will put My law in their minds, and write it on their hearts; and I will be their God, and they shall be My people. No more shall every man teach his neighbor, and every man his brother, saying, 'Know the Lord,' for they shall all know Me, from the least of them to the greatest of them, says the Lord. For I will forgive their iniquity, and their sin I will remember no more. (Jeremiah 31:31-34)

This was not the first covenant that God initiated; it is one of the last covenants he will make with mankind. This covenant foretold by Jeremiah is fulfilled with the establishment of the church of Christ as a new, better covenant as recorded by the writer of the book of Hebrews 8:7-13. Also note in verse 32 of this passage of Scripture from Jeremiah 31, "My covenant which they broke, though I was a husband to them, says the Lord." This is an early reference of God's relationship to his followers; the same relationship of Christ to the church, and the husband to the wife. In the New Testament we find that Jesus is the husband of the church (John 3:29) that he established and therefore has the same relationship to the church of Christ as God had to the children of Israel. We also find this same relationship between the husband and wife in a marriage (Matthew 19:5-6). We, as Christians, should pay much more attention to the sanctity of marriage because it is a model of God's and Jesus' relationship to their followers or those that believe in them and follow their commandments. Today, our society doesn't always hold marriage in the same high regard that the Scriptures tell us we should.

God made a covenant with Adam in Genesis 2:16-17 that he could partake of every tree in the garden except for the tree of the knowledge of good and evil. Adam and Eve promptly broke this covenant. He later made a covenant with Noah (Genesis 9:1-17) never to destroy the world again with water. God also made a covenant with Abram (Genesis 12:1-3) and then reinforced it with Isaac (Genesis 26:1-5) and Jacob (Genesis 28:13–22) to build and bless a great nation from their seed. God further sent the same message to the children of Israel through Moses (Exodus 19:5, 6) that he would make of them a great nation. They would be a special people, a treasure, a kingdom of priests, and a holy nation. This nation would exist until an earthly kingdom was established in the time of the Roman Empire. This was first promised in Genesis 3:15 and Luke writes of its fulfillment in Christ (Luke 1:68-79). Hebrews 9 contrasts God's old covenant or Old Testament with the children of Israel and the greater and more perfect tabernacle or new covenant or New Testament with a peculiar people. These peculiar people are Christians, members of the earthly kingdom, the church. This new covenant was ratified with Christ's blood (Hebrews 9:11-23). We remember it each time we partake of the Lord's Supper (I Corinthians 11:25). And, we are told that this covenant is everlasting (Hebrews 13:20). This worldly kingdom will exist until the world is destroyed and the church is delivered to God by Jesus (I Cor. 15:24). The Scriptures establish the eternity of the church of Christ.

We will only look at three terms that are used in the Old Testament to describe the church that Christ would establish—*kingdom, house,* and *temple*—due to the restrictions of time. However, I encourage you to closely examine the prophesies of the Old Testament concerning the Lord's church and how they are fulfilled in the New Testament.

The first term we look at is *kingdom*. Hundreds of years before the church of Christ was established, Daniel interprets a dream for the king and it's basically a forecast of coming kingdoms—earthly kingdoms that will arise—four of them (Daniel 2:39-45). As you look at the calendar of events from the time of Daniel forward, the fourth kingdom of Daniel's interpretation of the dream of Nebuchadnezzar would be established in the time of the third kingdom which was the Roman Empire. This fourth kingdom is the church of Christ. Daniel 2:44 states that in the time of those kings (the Roman Caesars) the God of heaven will set up a "kingdom" which shall never be destroyed, and it shall stand forever (Hebrews 13:20). Again, we see that the Scriptures foretell the eternity of this coming kingdom. The church of Christ or *kingdom of Christ* was established during that time of the Roman Empire (Acts 2) and it still exists today. This begs the question, "If the church of Christ was established during the Roman Empire, and it still exists today, why can't we recognize it from its scriptural description?" I'm afraid the answer is that mankind has tried to make the church of Christ something that God and Jesus did not intend and something that is influenced by man's worldly experiences and man's thirst for power. It has been institutionalized as we've brought in worldly influences and begun to adhere to tradition instead of the Scriptures even though Paul warned us not to do so in his letter to the church at Colosse (Colossians 2:8).

Ferguson (1999) writes that Clement has been cited as establishing organizational structure—"Christ-apostles-bishops and deacons" and Clement's writings are the earliest writings "presenting the idea of apostolic succession" (p. 168). This has led to the institution of a hierarchical structure to the church that has no basis in the first century church of Christ as depicted in the Scriptures.

Next we look at the term *house*. Isaiah uses the term *house* (Isaiah 2:1–5) to describe this future kingdom. He prophesied that in the last days, the mountain of the Lord's *house* would be established in Zion, the Old Testament word for Jerusalem. Luke 24:46–47 tells us, "Thus it is written, and thus it was necessary for the Christ to suffer and to rise from the dead the third day and the repentance and remissions of sins will be preached in his name to all nations, beginning in Jerusalem." The birth of the church of Christ in Jerusalem is the fulfillment of Isaiah 2 and its parallel passage in Micah 4. Micah said that many nations would come into the *house* of the Lord and this prophecy is fulfilled shortly after the church of Christ was established and the Word was taken to the Gentile nations by Peter and Paul. Isaiah's and Micah's prophesies are exactly what is described in Acts 2 when Peter preached the first sermon to the Israelites (Acts 2) and then later took the message to the Gentile Cornelius (Acts 10:23 ff). The church or the house of God was established and the law of the New Testament or the Word, the gospel or good news, begins to go forth from Jerusalem.

The third term used in the Old Testament that refers to the church that Christ would establish is *temple*. Zechariah (Zechariah 6:12–13) foretells that the branch would build the *temple* of the Lord. Jesus is identified as the branch in this passage as well as in Isaiah 11 and so is foretold to be the builder of the church. The church that he would build is referred to as the *temple* by Zechariah.

So we now have three terms used in the Old Testament referring to the church that would be established. Isaiah and Micah predicted the establishment of the *house* of the God; Daniel predicted the establishment of the *kingdom*; and Zechariah predicted the establishment of the *temple* and that the Branch or the Messiah or the Christ would build it. We find that these three terms in the Old Testament, *kingdom*, *temple*, and *house* are also used in the New Testament. There are additional terms found in the Scriptures that foretell of the establishment of the church and its fulfillment but I feel three are sufficient to make the point that the church was prophesized in the Old Testament and these prophesies were fulfilled in the New Testament.

The kingdom of heaven and the kingdom of God are used synonymously or interchangeably today to refer to heaven. But, the church is also the kingdom of God on earth. Look at Paul's usage in Colossians 1. Verse 13 states the fact that these brethren had been translated into the *kingdom of God*. Now look at verse 18 and verse 24—it is clearly stated here that the *body of Christ* is the *church of Christ*. So we have Paul the apostle using the terms body of Christ, kingdom of God, and church of Christ in one book, interchangeably, synonymously in referring to the same institution, the church of Christ or the Lord's church.

In I Timothy 3:15 Paul says, "The house of God is the church of God, the pillar and ground of the truth." We've already seen the word *kingdom* in Colossians 1:13 when we established in that book that the kingdom was the same thing as the church or body of Christ. The terms *household* and *temple* are also used in Ephesians 2:19–21. There are many other examples of different terms in both the Old Testament and the New Testament that refer to the church and I encourage you to look at additional passages to see that all of them are in harmony with each other.

But for now we see that the kingdom of God on earth today is the church of Christ or the Lord's church. It was established as recorded in Acts 2 on the day of Pentecost. From Acts 2 forward, the Lord began reigning and ruling over his kingdom. And Christians serve him willingly (Psalms 110:3) in the day of his power (Psalms 110:3) and he is ruling truly in the midst of his enemies (Psalms 110:2).

If we look around today, we find many groups calling themselves churches and they all claim to be the church of Christ as described in the New Testament. Brunner (1958) had this to say about this claim. "First of all, we must note an objective fact: all these various churches—the Roman Catholic as much as the Quakers—claim to be the true Church in the New Testament and finds therein the justification for its special characteristics" (p. 99). But a careful study of the Lord's church in the New Testament does not reveal many of the practices, ordinances, or doctrine that these various groups proclaim.

This is an abbreviated study of the prophesies of the church of Christ and I would certainly be remiss if I did not encourage you, the reader, to further study the Old Testament prophesies concerning the establishment of the church.

Chapter 2
The Establishment of the New Testament Church

"For this is my blood of the new covenant, which is shed for many for the remission of sins"
(Matthew 26:28).

Jesus brought a new covenant to earth and he talks about this new covenant when he initiates the Lord's supper as recorded by Matthew, "For this is my blood of the new covenant, which is shed for many for the remission of sins" (Matthew 26:28). This new covenant is the gospel of Christ and the establishment of the Lord's church. An examination of Daniel, Isaiah, and Zechariah foretell of the kingdom that will never be destroyed (Daniel 2:44), the house that will be established in the latter days (Isaiah 2: 1-5), and that the Branch will build the temple of the Lord (Zechariah 6). These terms kingdom, house, and temple all refer to the same thing—the church that Jesus would establish as the new covenant. This covenant replaces the covenant of the Old Testament with the children of Israel and brings God's grace and salvation to all peoples.

The church we want to examine is the church of Christ or Lord's church as described in the Scriptures. Today we find many usages for the word *church*. One of those usages is the designation of a place of worship or a building. A person may say, "Let's go to church" meaning to go to a specific building. Some will say, "Let's go to church" meaning to go to worship. Some also use church to denote a denomination such as the Baptist Church, the Catholic Church, the Methodist Church, and so forth. In the New Testament, the term is used to refer to a local congregation or to the body of Christ, the universal church. Scriptural references to the local church are seen in I Thessalonians 1:1, e.g., church of the Thessalonians, and several times in Revelation, e.g., church of Ephesus (Revelation 2:1). An example of a scriptural reference to the universal church or body of Christ is Colossians 1:18. "And He is the head of the body, the church, who is the beginning, the firstborn from the dead, that in all things He may have the preeminence."

The universal church is comprised of all Christians from the time of the establishment of the church until Jesus returns to gather all of his followers and take them to heaven. In the Scriptures, church is used to refer to the local congregation or to the universal church of Christ. It is not used to refer to buildings or to refer to various religious groups. The Greek word *ekklesia* translates church. Jesus uses it in Matthew 16:18 when he says, "...and on this rock I will build My church [ekklesia]. ...." Ekklesia never implies a building, but always a people. Its general meaning is *an assembly* or *a gathering* and its literal meaning is *the called out* and in Biblical times it was applied in general terms to people called to attend any type of public assembly. In this study I use this definition of church: a body of believers who are called out into a unified, loving covenant relationship with Jesus and with each other.

It is important that Christians know and understand what the church of Christ is and what it is not. We need to know where it began and by whose authority it exists. It is a matter of identity—we should be known as Christians, not by numerous other names. I have asked many people to tell me about their religious affiliation and they will say, "I am a Baptist" or "I am a Catholic" or some other denominational name, but the Scriptures do not use any of these terms to refer to Jesus' followers.

The church is essentially a fellowship of Jesus believing people, not an institution as man has made it. The reshaping of the church began in the second century after the death of Christ. In this fellowship of Jesus believing people, each individual has his or her special function or spiritual gift (Romans 12:3-8; I Corinthians 12:1-10; Ephesians 4:11-12; I Peter 4:10-11) without any hierarchy of rank. Jesus is the head; Christians are the body or the organism (I Corinthians 12:12-27).

Now let's go back to that Branch that would build the church. The Branch, in Zechariah 6, is a reference to Christ, the one who will build the kingdom or house or temple for this new covenant. This term *Branch* is also found in Isaiah 11 and other places in the Old Testament referring to the Messiah or the Christ (Zechariah 3:8; Zechariah 6:12). Jesus came to establish the church according to God's will and that is exactly what he did while here on the earth.

We will now look at some New Testament passages to determine when this church would be built. After all, this is where we find the kingdom or house or temple built—right down to the day and the hour of the day. As recorded in Mark 9:1, Jesus, before his death on the cross, said, "Assuredly, I say to you that there are some standing here who will not taste death till they see the kingdom of God present with power." Some people who were with him on that occasion would still be alive when the kingdom of God or church of Christ or the Lord's church would become a reality and they would see it come with power.

In Luke 24:45-49 we find an account of the promise of power to be bestowed on the apostles. I use the Gospel of Luke because he is also the author of Acts of the Apostles so there is that continuity between Luke's gospel account and the book of Acts. Verse 45 states, "And He opened their understanding, that they might comprehend the Scriptures." Isn't this a great passage? What would you give if Jesus or the Holy Spirit could come to you today and give you comprehension of the Scriptures? He can and does through his Word, the Scriptures. All one has to do is give the time to study and when studying, put away the influences of the world. Now let's go on with verses 46-49.

> Then He said to them, "Thus it is written, and thus it was necessary for the Christ to suffer and to rise from the dead the third day, and that repentance and remission of sins should be preached in His name to all nations, beginning in Jerusalem. Behold, I send the Promise of My Father upon you; but tarry in the city of Jerusalem until you are endued with power from on high."

At this point, the kingdom is still to come and it will come with power from on high. The kingdom will come in the lifetime of the apostles because they are instructed to tarry in Jerusalem until the power comes from on high. Jesus has set the mission of that church which was to come when he said, "...and that repentance and remission of sins should be preached in His name to all nations, beginning in Jerusalem." We will also see this commission to the apostles and consequently to all Christians in Matthew 28: 18-20.

Now let's examine this event of the birth of the church of Christ beginning with Acts 1:8. Jesus is talking to the apostles again and the apostles only when he says, "But you shall receive power when the Holy Spirit has come upon you; and you shall be witness to Me in Jerusalem, and in all Judea and Samaria, and to the end of the earth." Closely examine Acts 1: 1-7. Verse two states, "the apostles whom he had chosen." Note that from this point through Acts chapter two, every pronoun refers back to these apostles. They, the apostles, are told not to depart from Jerusalem but to wait for the promise of the Father. They, the apostles, would be "baptized with the Holy Spirit not many days from now" (Verse 5). The apostles are all named in verse thirteen. This baptism of power is not promised to all the disciples that had gathered in the upper room, but to the apostles only.

So we now have the apostles in the upper room, along with other disciples. Together, the apostles and disciples number about a hundred and twenty (Verse 15). Peter directs the selection of a replacement apostle for Judas and Matthias is selected (Verses 15-26) and he is now numbered with the eleven other apostles. This is an excellent example of decision making in the early church and it will be discussed in a subsequent chapter of this work.

Chapter two of Acts begins with them, the apostles, "with one accord in one place" (Verse 1). That "accord" is that they are waiting for the promise of the Father, to be "baptized with the Holy Spirit not many days from now" (Acts 1:5). They, the apostles, received this baptism of the Holy Spirit (Acts 2:2-4) and they, the apostles, began to speak in tongues. Verse four says the apostles, "began to speak as the Holy Spirit gave them utterance." This baptism of the Holy Spirit is in fulfillment of a lengthy section of Scripture in John 14, 15, and 16, where Jesus had promised the apostles that the Holy Spirit would come upon them and guide them into all truth, teach them all things, bring all things to their remembrance, and show them things to come. This has only occurred one other time in the Scriptures, and that is when Paul is blinded on the road to Damascus and is converted by Ananias in the city of Damascus. I often hear folks refer to Paul's conversion on the road to Damascus but he was not converted on the road to Damascus, but after he had followed Jesus' instructions and gone into the city and there he was converted by Ananias. This is the typical mistake we see in the church—we use terminology that is used over and over until it becomes tradition. Read this account in its entirety in Acts 9: 1-19.

Getting back to the baptism of the apostles by the Holy Spirit in the upper room, we find it's evident that this event came with much sound

(Acts 2:6), bringing the multitudes together so that everyone heard them, the apostles, "speak in his own language" (Acts 2:6). Peter preaches a sermon and some of the multitude were cut to their hearts and asked, "Men and brethren, what shall we do?" (Acts 2:37).

Peter's answer to them was, "Repent, and let every one of you be baptized in the name of Jesus Christ for the remission of sins; and you shall receive the gift of the Holy Spirit" (Acts 2:38). This promise was to all people (Verse 39) and those who received his Word were baptized and "that day about three thousand souls were added to the church" (Verse 41) according to the New King James Version.[1] This is very important. Prior to this time every reference to the kingdom, to the house, to the temple Jesus would build, was in the future tense. After this time every reference to the kingdom, to the house, to the temple, to the church, is in the past tense indicating that it, the church of Christ, the *house*, the *temple*, the *kingdom* has been born or established. We must also realize here that although the books of the New Testament are not in chronological order, the book of Acts was placed in the Scriptures before the epistles and Revelation so all references to the church in these books indicate that the church is already established.

We actually have the exact moment that the church was created. It was the day of Pentecost after Jesus was crucified (Acts 2:1) at the third hour of the day, nine o'clock in the morning (Verse 15). This is very important in studying the establishment of the church. We know that the church of Christ is in place from this point in time forward. Acts, chapters one and two, clearly give us this information. The church is also the kingdom referred to in Mark 9:1, "The kingdom will come with power." We have made three points: 1) the kingdom would come with power (Mark 9:1); 2) the power came with the Holy Spirit (Acts 1:8; Luke 24:45-49); and 3) this was all fulfilled on the day of Pentecost about nine o'clock in the morning (Acts 1 & 2). We now have the earthly church of Christ or kingdom of Christ or the first congregation of the Lord's established so now we will look at how one becomes a part or member of that church or kingdom that Christ established here on earth according to these Scriptures that we have available to us.

Aristides (abt 125 AD) described the early church in this manner:

1 Note: A better translation is "And day by day the Lord added to their number those who were being saved" (Acts 2:47b, NRSV) because the Greek *ekklesia* is not used here in Acts 2:47. Ekklesia is used in other places such as I Corinthians 1:2.

> The Christians, then, trace the beginning of their religion from Jesus the Messiah; and he is named the Son of God Most High. And it is said that God came down from heaven, and from a Hebrew virgin assumed and clothed himself with flesh; and the Son of God lived in a daughter of man. This is taught in the gospel, as it is called, which a short time was preached among them; and you also if you will read therein, may perceive the power which belongs to it. This Jesus, then, was born of the race of the Hebrews; and he had twelve disciples in order that the purpose of his incarnation might in time be accomplished. But he himself was pierced by the Jews, and he died and was buried; and they say that after three days he rose and ascended to heaven. Thereupon these twelve disciples went forth throughout the known parts of the world, and kept showing his greatness with all modesty and uprightness. And hence also those of the present day who believe that preaching are called Christians, and they are become famous. (Aristides, n,d,, II para. 4)

Aristides did not use any other term other than Christian to describe these believers of Christ. Other early documents, first century through the third century, reveal the same terminology used to describe believers and followers of Christ (Ferguson, 1999). Today many labels are used but those labels cannot be found in the New Testament church of Christ so wouldn't it seem logical that if we have become a Christian, we would want to called a Christian?

Entry into the Church

Gaining membership in the Lord's church is a very simple process if the pattern of the New Testament is followed. One gains membership in the church by only one way as recorded in the Book of Acts. When Peter preached the first sermon (Acts 2), the multitude responded with this question, "Men and Brethren, What shall we do?" (Acts 2:37). Peter's reply was, "Repent, and let every one of you be baptized in the name of Jesus Christ for the remission of sins; and you shall receive the gift of the Holy Spirit" (Acts 2:38). God added these first souls to the church after they were baptized. "Then those who gladly received his word were baptized; and that day about three thousand souls were added *to them*" (Acts 2:41) and verse 47 tells us, "And the Lord added to the church daily those who were being saved." A better translation of this verse is "added to the saved" because the word *ecclesia* is not used here.

Were there any prerequisites to being saved and added to the church? Sure there were. First, as we have stated earlier, Psalm 110:3 says, "Your people *shall* be volunteers in the day of Your power:" So we now know that the members of this organization, the church, gain entrance voluntarily, not by predestination, or by vote of the membership, but voluntarily of their own volition, and God, not man, adds them to the saved (Acts 2:47). There is no vote—it is between the individual and God. The second thing is that one must hear of Christ in order to have faith in him and to become a member of his church, the church of Christ. The multitudes had to hear the Word and they had to have faith in what they heard. These two things are the only prerequisites to being baptized and becoming a Christian; "So then faith *comes* by hearing, and hearing by the word of God" (Romans 10:17).Then those first Christians voluntarily repented and were baptized in the name of Jesus Christ for the remission of sins. Every *specific* account of salvation in the New Testament includes the act of baptism.

Were there any restrictions to the number of church members? The Bible says not. Again, we turn to Acts 2:39 and find in the words of Peter in his first sermon, "For the promise is to you and to your children, and to all who are afar off, as many as the Lord our God will call." Well, just how many will he call? Jesus himself tells us, as recorded by the disciple whom he loved, "And if anyone hears my words and does not believe, I will not judge him; for I did not come to judge the world but to save the world" (John 12:47). Jesus came to save the world. How many people are in the world? All of them! Jesus did not say that he came to save a specific number but he came to save all that would hear his Word, have faith in him, confess him before men, repent of their sins, and be baptized for the remission of their sins.

Peter wrote these words about who could be saved. "The Lord is not slack concerning *His* promise, as some count slackness, but is longsuffering toward us, not willing that any should perish but that all should come to repentance" (II Peter 3:9). So we find that the will or desire of the establisher of the church of Christ is that all would come to be saved, but sorrowfully, we know that not all who hear the gospel will do so.

Colossians 3 contains a very apt description of what one is before accepting Christ and what one should be after accepting Christ. I strongly recommend reading that passage often and use the reading of it to reflect about yourself and how you are doing as a vital member of the body of Christ. God's book is full of good everyday instruction if we will but take the time to read and study. How can a Christian know what he or she is supposed to do, what to believe, unless they study God's Word?

Understanding of the Scriptures comes with study and sometimes with the help of another individual. Remember the account of the Ethiopian eunuch and Philip in Acts 8:26-39. Philip is sent by an angel to intercept the eunuch as he was returning to Ethiopia after having been in Jerusalem to worship. The eunuch was reading from Isaiah when Philip joined him and asked, "Do you understand what you are reading?" The eunuch's reply was "How can I unless someone guides me."

Philip began to preach Jesus to him. They came upon water by the wayside and the eunuch asked Philip "See, *here is* water. What hinders me from being baptized?" Philip's answer to that question was "If you believe with all your heart you may." How simple is that. The eunuch has heard the Word, he has faith in what the Word says, and he confesses "I believe that Jesus Christ is the Son of God."

Now pay close attention here—the inspired account of this event states, "And both Philip and the eunuch went down into the water, and he baptized him. Now when they came up out of the water, the Spirit of the Lord caught Philip away, so that the eunuch saw him no more; and he went on his way rejoicing." How could they have gone down into the water and come up out of the water if there was not sufficient water to immerse the eunuch? Baptism is immersion and it happens immediately after hearing and having faith in the Word of Christ, repenting, and confessing one's belief in what he/she has heard. Review the examples of conversion in the Book of Acts. Not all conversion accounts offer these steps, if you will, but some portion of them, so if one compiles the actions that take place during these conversion accounts in the book of Acts one will find all these elements—hearing, believing, repenting, confessing Christ, and being baptized—when one is added to the church of Christ as described in the Bible. Test it. All it takes is a little time and a Bible.

Baptism is commanded (Acts 10:48), baptism is for the remission of sins (Acts 2:38), it was authorized by Jesus (Mark 16:16), and baptism saves (I Peter 3:21). These are not the only passages that teach these things about baptism but are a good starting point if you want to begin a study on that subject.

The universal church is composed of all those believers that have been baptized in Jesus' name for the remission of their sins since the church was established on Pentecost as recorded in Acts chapter one and two. It will also include all those in the future who come to be baptized in Jesus' name for the remission of their sins.

Paul informed the church of Christ at Corinth that they should speak the same thing, there should be no divisions in the church of Christ, and that they should be in the same mind and in the same judgment (I Corinthians 1:10). The Corinthians church had some internal contentions and Paul is writing to instruct them in keeping the Word that they had been taught. Wouldn't it be great today if all organizations that call themselves Christian would speak the same thing, that there were no divisions among them, and that they were of the same mind and the same judgment? In Jesus' prayer in the garden, he specifically prayed that his disciples at that time and in the future would be as one as he and God are one. These are his words, "Now I am no longer in the world, but these are in the world, and I come to You. Holy Father, keep through Your name those whom You have given Me, that they may be one as We *are*" (John 17:8).

In this chapter we've read how the church was established in the Scriptures, how members of the church were added by God, and what we can learn about entry into this church of Christ. In the next chapter we will look at the church of Christ in more detail as an organism first, and second, with organizational aspects necessary to carry out the various ministries of the church.

Based on my examination of the church in the New Testament, when one examines the first century church and today's Christian groups, I recommend and support these particular words of C. B. Hassell (1886).

> The church of the first century forms the standard and example for the church of all future ages. Should there exist now on earth a body of professed Christians who occupy the same ground in faith and practice of the church of the first century, they are RIGHT; and if any should be found occupying a different position, they are WRONG. The true church of Christ and false or merely nominal churches are to be distinguished by a comparison with the apostolic standard. (pp. 269-270)

Chapter 3
The Organism, the Organization

"Unless the Lord *builds the house, They labor in vain who build it;"*
(Psalms 127:1a).

Organizations are governed by visions of their leadership; mission statements that focus on goals; and rules, bylaws, and doctrines set forth in constitutions. All these things, discussed later in this work, are provided to the church from one source—God's Word, the Bible (2 Timothy 3:16-17). This chapter examines the first century Christian's perception of the church. It further sets forth evidence that the true church is actually an organism.

This chapter consists of three points: 1) the Bible is the inspired Word of God; 2) the church is an organism; and 3) the church has some organizational structure but it is secondary to the organism. I will also discuss briefly the hierarchy of the church.

The Bible is the Inspired Word of God

The Bible was inspired, "God-breathed." It is not the thoughts of those who wrote it (2 Timothy 3:16; 2 Peter 1:20-21). Autonomous congregations of the Lord do not need men's constitutions and bylaws. Christian groups governed by men's laws differ from the church set forth in the New Testament. [Note: Comments regarding 2 Peter 1:20 might be misleading. "Private interpretation" does not refer to the reader's interpretation, but as v 21 explains, the writer's (Peter) interpretation.]

In Paul's words: "All scripture *is* given by inspiration of God, and *is* profitable for doctrine, for reproof, for correction, for instruction in righteousness, that the man of God may be complete, thoroughly equipped for every good work" (II Timothy 3: 16-17).

Jesus himself makes reference to and endorses the inspiration of God:

> While the Pharisees were gathered together, Jesus asked them, saying, "What do you think about the Christ? Whose Son is He?" They said to him, "*The Son of* David."
>
> And He said to them, "How then does David in the Spirit call Him *'Lord,'* saying: *'The Lord said to my Lord, "Sit at my right hand, Till I make your enemies Your footstool"* '?
>
> "If David then calls Him *'Lord,'* how is He his Son?" (Matthew 22:41-45)

Jesus is quoting from Psalm 110 in this passage and his reference to the phrase, "in the Spirit," indicates inspiration of the Holy Spirit. Jesus is talking about himself here and quoting Psalm 110 so it has to refer to whom—Jesus Christ. He is affirming that Psalm 110 is referring to him and at the same time verifying that the Scriptures are inspired.

As a sidebar, Psalm 110 (NKJV) also says in verse 3, "Your people shall be volunteers in the day of Your power:" so we now know that the members of this organization, the church gain entrance voluntarily, not by predestination, not by birth, or by vote, but voluntarily. AND—God adds them to those that have already been saved. "And day by day the Lord added to their number those who were being saved" (Acts 2:47b, NRSV). Christians are added to the others that had been saved as they obeyed the call of the gospel. Some translations read "added to the church", but the Greek word ekklesia is not used here. It is used in many other New Testament passages in references to the church; for example, I Corinthians.

Peter also writes of this inspiration of the Holy Spirit in the Scriptures when he said, "for prophecy never came by the will of man, but holy men of God spoke *as they were* moved by the Holy Spirit" (II Peter 1:21.

Peter also tells us that "no prophecy of scripture is of any private interpretation" (II Peter 1:20). The inspired writer, Peter, tells us that the Bible is the inspired Word of God and that the prophecy of the Scriptures are not for private interpretation nor was God's Word interpreted by the writers of it. That must mean that one such as I, unschooled in the Bible except for my own study, can read and understand God's Word without having to have interpretation from another individual. However, in my early studies, I was guided by other individuals and by the "traditional" sermons I heard but now I make every effort to adhere simply to the teaching and doctrine that is found in God's Word. When I hear new lessons from the Scriptures, it is my responsibility to revisit them by studying God's Word.

The Church Is an Organism

Next, many believers today view the church as an organization, but we need to ask the question, "Is the church of Christ, as described in the Scriptures, really an organization?" To answer this question I borrow a definition of organization from the secular world where we find that, "An *organization* is a stable system of individuals who work together to achieve common goals through a hierarchy of ranks and divisions of labor" (Emphasis in the original; Rogers, 1995, p. 375). From this definition, we see that the church does have aspects of an organization. When I write about the organizational aspect of the church of Christ, Rogers' definition best describes what I am writing about. From an organizational perspective, we would hope that congregations of the church of Christ are stable systems of individuals and we would hope that they work together to achieve common goals.

But, most importantly, the church of Christ is first and foremost an organism in the way it functions. We seldom if ever view the church as an organism except when someone might be presenting a lesson or sermon using this term but we do not allow this term, *organism,* to be our framework of the structure of the church of Christ. We allow the world view of an organization to dominate our thoughts of how the church is organized structurally. That is because man has over the centuries institutionalized the church. We need to return to Paul's description of the church of Christ that he used when he wrote to the Corinthians:

> For as the body is one and has many members, but all the members of that one body, being many, are one body, so also *is* Christ. For by one Spirit we were all baptized into one body—whether Jews or Greeks, whether slaves or free—and have all been made to drink into one Spirit. For in fact the body is not one member but many.

> If the foot should say, "Because I am not a hand, I am not of the body," is it therefore not of the body? And if the ear should say, "Because I am not an eye, I am not of the body," is it therefore not of the body? If the whole body *were* an eye, where *would be* the hearing? If the whole *were* hearing, where *would be* the smelling? But now God has set the members, each one of them, in the body just as He pleased. And if they *were* all one member, where *would* the body *be?*
>
> But now indeed *there are* many members, yet one body. And the eye cannot say to the hand, "I have no need of you"; nor again the head to the feet, "I have no need of you." No, much rather, those members of the body which seem to be weaker are necessary. And those *members* of the body which we think to be less honorable, on these we bestow greater honor; and our unpresentable *parts* have greater modesty, but our presentable *parts* have no need. But God composed the body, having given greater honor to that *part* which lacks it, that there should be no schism in the body, but *that* the members should have the same care for one another. And if one member suffers, all the members suffer with *it;* or if one member is honored, all the members rejoice with *it.*
>
> Now you are the body of Christ, and members individually. (I Corinthians 12:12-27)

I included the entire passage of Scripture here because it is very important for the reader to read and understand that Paul's description of the church of Christ is clearly that of an organism. He uses that term again in Romans 12:4-5 and in other passages of Scripture. The Merriam-Webster Online Dictionary defines an organism as "a complex structure of interdependent and subordinate elements whose relationships and properties are largely determined by their function in the whole" (retrieved April 17, 2004 from www.m-w.com). Through the pages of this book we will examine what the Scriptures tell us about this organism, the church of Christ, how its elements are dependent upon each other, which elements are subordinate to which elements, and how their functions maintain the whole organism of the church. I have surveyed many individuals and about 95% of them have never considered the perspective of the church of Christ as an organism, even those who associate themselves with the congregations that call themselves "church of Christ."

So, having said all that, we do not find any dichotomy in these two terms describing the church and that the two terms, *organism* and *organization*, work together in well performing congregations of the church of Christ. However, we need to keep in mind that the organism is a much more important aspect of the church than the organization and that the organization comes into play as we engage ourselves in the various ministries of the church.

Remember, the world shapes many of our paradigms and organizational structure is one of them—most people see the church as an organization but they don't see the organism! In the world in which we live and work, we see businesses and other enterprises structured in some sort of hierarchy, generally a top-down structure. We see military groups as organizations and how they are top-down in organizational structure. We become accustomed to these hierarchies and they mold our paradigms about how any organization ought to be structured. Without thinking we bring this paradigm into the church and it overshadows the organism of the Scriptures. Therefore, we have institutionalized the church by our acceptance of this traditional organization structural paradigm from our worldly experiences.

In the surveys I conducted with members of Christian groups, more than 80% of those who participated, depicted the church in a hierarchal manner similar to the one shown in Figure 3.1. Less than 5% of the participants actually depicted the church as an organism. The other 15% depicted the structure in various ways that did not reveal any additional models worthy of consideration in this study. When participants were asked why their perspectives of the structure of the church were shown in such a fashion, they all responded that it's the way organizations are always structured.

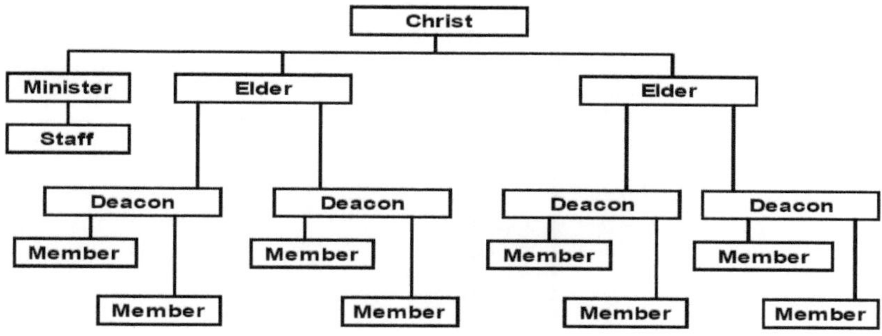

Figure 3.1 - A Typical Structure of the Church

What you see in Figure 3.1 is the typical organizational structure that you see in the military, in businesses, and in other types of organizations. The migrations of the church as an organism to that of an organization started before the scriptural church of Christ had been established for very long. Paul warned against this very infiltration of worldly views into the church in Colossians 2:8 when he wrote, "Beware lest anyone cheat you through philosophy and empty deceit, according to the tradition of men, according to the basic principles of the world, and not according to Christ."

This hierarchal type of structure is designed to restrict the involvement, behavior, action, and function of those who make up the members of such an organization, and to give hierarchal power to those in leading positions. This begs me to ask, "How did we get from the organism described in God's Scriptures to this organizational structure that most people who identify themselves as Christians think of when asked about the structure of the church?"

The answer has been given by Bible scholars, church historians, and theologians, but they are largely unheard because those in control of various religious groups don't want to give up their power. They don't want to be servant leaders and follow God's Word. Most of our congregational members are so caught up in their individual lives that they don't want to make the time to really examine the Scriptures without the biases and prejudices called traditions that we've inherited from our fathers.

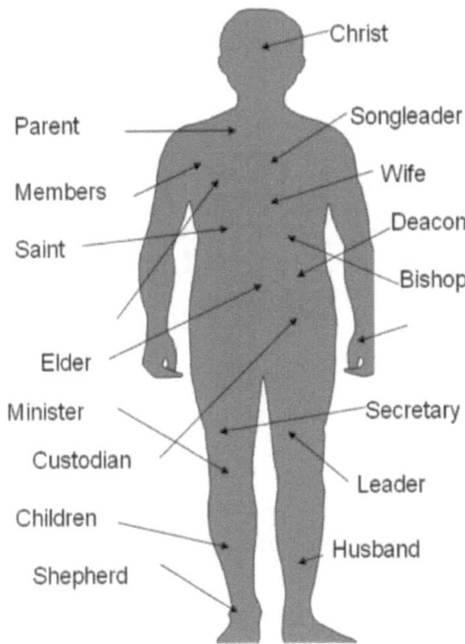

Figure 3.2 – The Organism

A depiction of the church as an organism is that of a body with all the parts equal in importance (Fair, 1996, p. 264; Richards & Hoeldtke, 1980, p. 98) as shown in Figure 3.2 – The Organism. This depiction is based on Paul's description in I Corinthians 12:12-31 of the church as an organism.

As already discussed in the Introduction to this study, James Moffatt (1938), Washburn Professor of Church History at Union Theological Seminary, gives us insight to what was occurring in the church leadership during its infancy. Toward the end of the first century of the existence of the church, a "mono-episcopate" [head elder] began to emerge out of the presbyters [eldership]. Moffatt found no clear reason for this phenomenon which started in Syria and Asia Minor. As this leadership model developed, the church's organizational structure came to be a bishop over the congregation or collection of congregations, the eldership moved to the second tier of leadership, and deacons or assistants became the third tier of congregational ministry. This practice was not common during the time of Ignatius and there were no such leadership structures in Philippi, Corinth, or Rome until later (pp. 44 - 45); however, Ignatius of Antioch (37 – 105) was instrumental in the shift in church functioning to organizational patterns of the Greco-Roman culture of the time (Ferguson, 1999). The "Why?" of it has not been discovered. Ignatius was known as a disciple of the Apostle John and some religious groups trace their apostolic lineage back to Ignatius as the third pope of their particular religious group.

At the time of Ignatius, the one-bishop rule had not caught on in regions other than Syria and Asia Minor, but according to Bruce (1958) and Lightfoot (1898) the one-bishop rule or model was firmly entrenched in most churches. By the end of the third century, one-bishop rule prevailed everywhere (Knox, 1956).

It is very important to understand that the church is an organism and as such all the parts are equal; however, each part has a unique role or function based on the gifts that we read about in I Corinthians 12:12-31. Christians need to remember that the "more excellent way" is the exercise of love as Paul discussed in I Corinthians 13. This perspective on the equality of the members of the church as an organism does not take anything away from those in scripturally correct ministries or functions of the church, whether it is a minister, elder (bishop, shepherd, or pastor), a deacon, or any other member who is using his or her gifts according to God's Word.

The Church has some Organizational Structure

But the church is also an organization. There is no dichotomy here! The church does have components of an organization but it is also has the characteristics of an organism and those characteristics should be prevalent in Christian groups today, but I have not found this to be true in my surveys. In later chapters, we will examine the organization and the organism and not separate them but learn how the two frameworks come together and how, when they do come together, the church grows, God is glorified, and the members are all with one accord.

An example of the need for some organizational structure is when special servants were selected in Acts 6:1-6. They were selected to take care of those Hellenistic widows who were being neglected. They had to have some organization in order to carry out that ministry just as any ministry in the church today needs some organization to carry out its ministry—the lesson I'm stressing is that we need to restore our attitude of the church as an organism and put much less emphasis on the organization. The various parts of an organism work together to perform the overall function of the particular organism.

I want it to be clear to the reader that this writer believes that a congregation could operate with a minimum of members and without any formal functional positions (elders, deacons, teachers, ministers, and so forth) because all the members of this body or organism are all commanded to perform the same basic function in the church (Matthew 28:18-20). This is how many congregations begin. All a congregation needs are a few members who are willing to carry out the work of the church according to God's Word and it can function just as a fully matured congregation with such functional roles of elders, deacons, teachers, ministers, and so forth. It just will not be as effective because it will not have all the resources that come to bear when a congregation is truly organized and functioning as described in God's Word. To be a scripturally structured and mature organism, these interdependent, functional, and subordinate elements (elders, deacons, teachers, ministers, and so forth) need to be put in place within the congregation of the Lord as soon as members are scripturally mature and capable of taking on these vital functions.

Remember, our perspectives are influenced by our families, the societies where we live, businesses where we work, and the teachers (both religious and secular) we have had in our life. Ask yourself, as a Christian shouldn't the greatest influence to shape your view of the church of Christ, its organization, and its leadership come from God's Word? Are you willing to change your view of the church of Christ, its organization, and its leadership if the evidence for this change comes from God's Word?

In today's religious world, the respective views of the leaders and followers of the organized churches may vary. People act, not according to how the church (organism) was intended to be, but how church leaders say it is and according to how they think it ought to be based on their respective paradigms. Those paradigms are shaped by our experiences in worldly organizations and enterprises; therefore, today's church leaders do not necessarily follow the pattern or the plan of the church as depicted in the New Testament but they follow those dictates, traditions, or models that man has put in place over the centuries.

Mankind has created alternate meanings of the church—the organization that Jesus Christ created. To get the proper view of the church that we should have alive and viable today, the church that Jesus Christ created, we need to examine what God's Word tells us about the church of Christ, its organization, and its leadership. In order to do that we need to examine what both the Old Testament and the New Testament disclose to us when we study them without bias.

What's happening in the world is being reflected in the church today and has been for several centuries. We need to reaffirm to ourselves who God is and be assured of that as John the Baptist was in Matthew 3. John the Baptist knew who he was and he knew who Jesus was and he understood their relationship. Christians today need to understand who they are and who Jesus is and the relationship they should have with him.

Hierarchy of the Church

Congregations are to be autonomous. Elders or pastors or shepherds or bishops function as the overseers of the congregations in spiritual and scriptural matters. Deacons function to perform specific duties within the congregation. All members of the congregation have unique functions, roles, and responsibilities. We would call these spiritual gifts (Ephesians 4:7-16; Romans 12). However, all Christians have the responsibility to do the work of the church.

Christ is the head of the church. We read in Ephesians 1:22,23 "And He put all things under His feet and gave Him to be head over all things to the church, which is His body, the fullness of Him who fills all in all." Colossians 1:24 states, "I now rejoice in my sufferings for you, and fill up in my flesh what is lacking in the afflictions of Christ, for the sake of His body, which is the church."

The elders' function is to oversee the spiritual aspects of the local congregations. Christ designated this functional role as written by the apostle Paul in Ephesians 4:11, "And He Himself gave some to be apostles, some prophets, some evangelists, and some pastors [elders] and teachers." We know the duties of elders because they are described by the apostle Peter in I Peter 5:1-4, "The elders who are among you I exhort, I who am a fellow elder and a witness of the sufferings of Christ, and also a partaker of the glory that will be revealed: Shepherd the flock of God which is among you, serving as overseers, not by compulsion but willingly, not for dishonest gain but eagerly; nor as being lords over those entrusted to you, but being examples to the flock; and when the Chief Shepherd appears, you will receive the crown of glory that does not fade away."

Every congregation of the Lord's church should have elders (Acts 14:23; Titus 1:5) whenever there are men that can fulfill that office. Paul describes the qualities that elders should possess in Titus 1:5-9. That passage reads:

> "For this reason I left you in Crete, that you should set in order the things that are lacking, and appoint elders

> in every city as I have commanded you—if a man is blameless, the husband of one wife, having faithful children not accused of dissipation or insubordination. For a bishop must be blameless, as a steward of God, not self-willed, not quick-tempered, not given to wine, not violent, not greedy for money, but hospitable, a lover of what is good, sober-minded, just, holy, self-controlled, holding fast the faithful word as he has been taught, that he may be able, by sound doctrine, both to exhort and convict those who contradict."

Elders are also called pastors (Ephesians 4:11), shepherds (I Peter 5:2-4), rulers (Hebrews 13:17), bishops or overseers (Acts 20:28; I Timothy 3:1-7) depending on the function of the elder that is being addressed by the inspired writer of God's Word (Ferguson, 1999). We will talk about elders and their function as ministers in more detail when we discuss their leadership role in spiritual matters in the church.

There is also a need for someone to head up the various ministries in which a congregation decides it wants to participate. Seven men were first selected to look after the widows who were being neglected in the early days of the church so that the apostles could look after the spiritual well being of the young church. Although the Scriptures never identify these seven men as deacons, we have come to look at the following passage as the example of deacon selection in the first century church.

> "Now in those days, when the number of the disciples was multiplying, there arose a complaint against the Hebrews by the Hellenists, because their widows were neglected in the daily distribution. Then the twelve summoned the multitude of the disciples and said,
>
> "It is not desirable that we should leave the word of God and serve tables. Therefore, brethren, seek out from among you seven men of good reputation, full of the Holy Spirit and wisdom, whom we may appoint over this business: but we will give ourselves continually to prayer and to the ministry of the word." And the saying pleased the whole multitude. And they chose Stephen, a man full of faith and the Holy Spirit, and Philip, Prochorus, Nicanor, Timon, Parmenas, and Nicolas, a proselyte from Antioch,

> whom they set before the apostles; and when they had prayed, they laid hands on them." (Acts 6:1-6)

There should also be deacons in every congregation of the Lord's church (Philippians 1:1) that has men that exhibit the scriptural qualities and their duties can be found in I Timothy 3:8-13. So we have Christ as head of the church, we have elders to oversee the spiritual needs of the flock, and we have deacons to see after the work of the congregation. Does this mean members of the congregation cannot be involved in the work of the church? No, remember the organism. All members can and must support the work of the congregation by helping the deacons and elders as opportunity affords itself. Congregations desiring to be scriptural in all respects should have elders and deacons if there are men in the congregation who have the qualities for these functions as described in the New Testament. If there aren't men with those qualities, the minister or preacher should be developing them such as Paul instructed Timothy. Congregations that are scriptural as defined by God's Word will grow and prosper in today's chaotic world.

It's important for every Christian to study God's Word to understand the structure and organization of the church of Christ for the following reasons:

- It's God's will and it's his Word.
- When the church functioned as an organism it enjoyed immense growth.
- Proper perspective of the church as an organism allows Christians to use their spiritual gifts (functions) unbridled by hierarchy.
- It allows the church, that body of believers who are called out into a unified, loving, covenant relationship with Jesus and with each other to carry forth the mission of the church (Matthew 28:18-20).
- Jesus warned against a hierarchical form of leadership (Matthew 20: 25-28, 23:8-12; Luke 22:25-27; Mark 10:42ff).

Chapter 4
The Head of the Lord's Church

"And He put all things under His feet, and gave Him to be head over all things to the church, which is His body, the fullness of Him who fills all in all" (Ephesians 1:22-23).

When we see and hear a great musical band performing, we automatically think, "It must have a great band director." When we see a successful business venture, we say, "It must have a great leader as CEO or president." When we hear of great military victories, we attribute the victory to the generals. To examine any successful venture, the observer must first examine the quality and character of its leader. The church is not any different. When we look at a group through the lens of organizational development to determine what it is about, we get the best indicator by examining the leadership. Why? Because the leader sets the culture of the group. The culture of a group is how the members of the group do things. Culture is defined as "those learned behaviors characterizing the total way of life of members within any given society" (Hughes, Ginnett, & Curphy, 2006, p. 151). Within the culture of society, we have subcultures and organizational or group cultures. An observer would examine the culture of the church as a group culture, defined as "a system of shared backgrounds, norms, values, or beliefs among members of a group" (Hughes, et al., 2006, p. 346).

Christians' shared background would simply be our faith in Jesus Christ as our Lord and Savior. We have a mutual belief in Jesus Christ as our Lord, our Savior, and our Mediator. Our norms, our values, and our beliefs should all have a common source—the Holy Scriptures—because that is where we hear the words of Jesus Christ today.

As we begin the examination of the leadership of the Lord's church, we must first examine its head, Jesus Christ, and his leadership style and leadership characteristics keeping in mind that he sets the tone for the church's culture or the way we do things. This is important because present day religious leaders should be emulating Jesus and the culture he established as they fulfill their leadership roles and functions in their respective congregations.

Jesus began to reveal some glimpse of the church with these words:

> "Then Jesus spoke to the multitudes and to His disciples, saying: "The scribes and the Pharisees sit in Moses' seat. Therefore whatever they tell you to observe, *that* observe and do, but do not do according to their works; for they say, and do not do. For they bind heavy burdens, hard to bear, and lay *them* on men's shoulders; but they *themselves* will not move them with one of their fingers. But all their works they do to be seen by men. They make their phylacteries broad and enlarge the borders of their garments. They love the best places at feasts, the best seats in the synagogues, greetings in the marketplaces, and to be called by men, 'Rabbi, Rabbi.' But you, do not be called 'Rabbi'; for One is your Teacher, the Christ, and you are all brethren. Do not call anyone on earth your father; for One is your Father, He who is in heaven. And do not be called teachers; for One is your Teacher, the Christ. But he who is greatest among you shall be your servant. (Matthew 23:1-11)

Jesus is telling the multitude and his disciples that there is to be a new society or a new way of behavior and action with God's people. They are all to be brethren under one teacher and under one God and that the prevalent leadership style will be that of a servant leader. This new covenant would be different than it was under the Law. The leaders of the Jews did not exercise the godly qualities that they taught about the Law so Jesus said to do what they said but do not look to them as examples. The indication is that Jesus' followers are to do as they say they will do when they accept Jesus as their Lord and Savior.

This same message is given to us by the inspired writer Mark when James and John came and asked to sit on Jesus' right and left hand:

> "And when the ten heard *it,* they began to be greatly displeased with James and John. But Jesus called them to *Himself* and said to them, 'You know that those who are considered rulers over the Gentiles lord it over them, and their great ones exercise authority over them. Yet it shall not be so among you; but whoever desires to become great among you shall be your servant. And whoever of you desires to be first shall be slave of all. For even the Son of Man did not come to be served, but to serve, and to give His life a ransom for many.'" (Mark 10:42-45)

Again Jesus tells his disciples that the new rulers or leaders will not Lord or exercise authority over people but they are to act and behave as servant leaders. Also read Matthew 20:25-28 and Luke 22:25-27.

"The hierarchal 'headship' pattern of leadership demonstrated so clearly in the Old Testament Israel, does not find expression in the New Testament" (Richards & Hoeldtke, 1980, p. 17). In the Old Testament we saw headships exhibited in the patriarchs, the judges, and the kings that ruled over God's chosen people. In the New Testament that same usage of headship cannot be found because Jesus is the head of the body (Ephesians 1:22; 4:15-16; Colossians 1:18). "... The function of the head of a body can never be 'delegated' to other parts of the body" (Richards & Hoeldtke, 1980, p. 17).

The inspired writer Paul wrote to the church at Colosse these words, "And He is the head of the body, the church, who is the beginning, the firstborn from the dead, that in all things He may have the preeminence" (Colossians 1:18). The Hebrew writer also said that Jesus was "the author and finisher of our faith" (Hebrews 12:2) and described him as the High Priest (Hebrews 5). The Romans, Pharisees, Sadducees, and Scribes all had traditional or position power but Jesus had authority. Authority is legitimate or authentic leadership and it is influential.

Modern day scholar of leadership, Warren Bennis (1989) writes that "there are three basic reasons why leaders are important" (p. 15). First, the effectiveness of the organization is dependent on the leader. We can look at the world today and see that Jesus was certainly effective in bringing the church into being because it has survived these two thousand years and has hundreds of millions of followers.

Second, the organization's leader must provide stability or a guiding purpose to the organization. We will see that Jesus did that and did it very well during his ministry on earth and continues to do so through his Word that has been brought down through the ages in the Holy Scriptures. Any deviation from his leadership and hence his Word comes from mankind.

And third, the leader must exemplify integrity. As we examine Jesus Christ, the head of the Lord's church, we will find that he does all these things and that he wants his followers to continue in his example. He spent three years training his leadership team and all the time he "walked the talk" that he was teaching them.

When Jesus began his ministry here on earth, the first thing he did was look up his cousin John the Baptist in the wilderness of Judea where John was baptizing folks for the repentance of sin in preparation for the coming of the Messiah (Matthew 3). Jesus came to the Jordan River to be baptized by John and at first John resisted and questioned him, "I need to be baptized by You, and are You coming to me?" (v. 14). Jesus answered and said to John, "permit it to be so now, for thus it is fitting for us to fulfill all righteousness" (v. 15).

By this very first public act of the beginning of his recorded ministry, Jesus was setting an example of the importance of baptism to all his followers. If he as the leader of this upcoming Christian church needed to be baptized, then his followers need to be baptized as well. The necessity of baptism became clearer to his followers (Acts 2) then and should be evident to Christians today.

As Jesus came up out of the water after baptism, the heavens opened and "He saw the Spirit of God descending like a dove and alighting on Him." And a mighty voice came from heaven saying, "This is my Beloved Son, in whom I am well pleased" (Matthew 3:16-17). God is proclaiming to the world that this is his Son Jesus Christ. At the same time he is legitimizing him or empowering him to do God's will here on earth. Jesus expresses to his followers that this is his mission. "For I have come down from heaven, not to do My own will, but the will of Him who sent Me" (John 6:38).

In the fourth chapter of Matthew we find that immediately after baptism Jesus was led by the Spirit into the wilderness and there he was tempted by the devil. It is recorded that the devil tempted Jesus three times, and three times Jesus responded with a Scripture. From the perspective of a leader, Jesus was maintaining and demonstrating to his followers the value he placed in the Scriptures during this time of temptation while remaining true to his mission, to do the will of his father (John 4:34). He is doing as all good leaders do or as we often hear today, "He is walking the talk." He is the example!

In Matthew 4:17, Matthew writes, "From that time Jesus began to preach and to say, "Repent, for the kingdom of heaven is at hand." Jesus, the head of the Lord's church is setting the vision for his followers. As he dwelt here on earth and worked with his disciples he continued that message. He was consistent in that message and that is one of the things church leaders should be doing today. They should be consistent in keeping Jesus' vision of the kingdom of heaven before their respective congregations.

Thus far, Jesus has set examples in baptism and in maintaining the Scriptures as the source of encouragement when we are under attack from the evil one. He has also established his mission while here on the earth and set a vision or goal for his followers. Now let's look at his actions or his performance as a leader.

The very next thing that Jesus did was start to pick his leadership team; those folks that were going to carry on his work after he was gone—those folks that were going to continue to teach those things he taught them during the three years of his earthly ministry to do his Father's will. He then spent the next three years training them. There's a very valuable lesson here in leadership development that we will touch on in other parts of this book, but this is a very valuable lesson that Christian groups may be missing today—lack of rigor in leadership training that is consistent with Jesus and his Word.

All the time he was here on earth Jesus was proclaiming the gospel, preaching, and healing the sick. As great multitudes begin to follow him, he seized the opportunity to teach them what we commonly call the beatitudes in his sermon on the mount. He starts this teaching or training by telling them how they are to act as his followers (Matthew 5:1-16). In the following few verses he tells them that he has come not to destroy the Law that has been their guidance for centuries but to fulfill prophesies that are contained in that the Old Testament.

He then gets very specific about some of the actions that they should not do such as murder, commit adultery, divorce, swear, and take matters in their own hands or retaliate against others when they feel they've been wronged (Matthew 5: 20-42). And then he tells them about love—agape love—and how the practice of agape love is perfection for his followers because his Father is perfect in loving us.

Then Jesus goes into a lesson on how his followers should do their charitable deeds (Matthew 6:1-4) and how they are to pray (Matthew 6: 5-15). He talks to them about fasting (Matthew 6:16-18) and about how to deal with earthly wealth (Matthew 6:19-34), and that's a real lesson we could all learn from today but we tend to ignore it. He concludes the lesson on wealth with a plea to seek first the kingdom of God and his righteousness and all these material things that we need will be added to or given to us.

His next lesson is about judging others (Matthew 7:1-6) and then he shows a quality that we always look for in leaders—he motivates his listeners (Matthew 7:7-11). He tells them that they are the salt of the earth and that they are a light unto the world. He then lays out that golden rule or rule of behavior for his followers (Matthew 7:12). He tells them there are two ways of life. One way will get you to that vision of Heaven, and the other way leads to destruction (Matthew 7:13-14). He then gives these followers some warnings that are still relevant to Christians today. False teachers will come in among his followers and try to lead them astray and that not everyone that calls him Lord will enter the kingdom of heaven (again emphasizing the vision) but only those that do the will of God will enter that promised land of heaven (Matthew 7:15-23). Jesus concludes this first comprehensive lesson that is recorded in the Scriptures with some instruction on how to plan our association with him. This rock that he tells his followers to build on is faith in him (Matthew 7:24-27; Matthew 16: 17-19).

The next very important lesson he teaches his followers is to not do things for personal recognition. In chapter 8, Matthew tells us the story of Jesus healing the leper and then he asks the leper not to tell the story because Jesus as a leader is not seeking recognition for himself but he is seeking recognition for God, our Father and our Creator. Leaders today, both in religious groups and in the secular world, should learn from this if they truly want to serve the organization in which they are positioned as a leader. There's a sidebar lesson in this scenario in that Jesus was always responsive to the need of the moment. He healed when the sick were brought to him. He turned water into wine at the wedding feast. He fed the multitudes when they were hunger, and there are numerous writings about him serving others as the need was demonstrated. Isn't that a great lesson! When is the best time to look for the lost sheep? As soon as it's apparent that they're lost. When is the best time to feed or clothe someone? When they have the need. Shouldn't all church leaders and followers of Jesus today take that lesson and put it into practice throughout their respective Christian groups?

I realize we've covered a lot of territory thus far in this chapter and also realize that this is not a comprehensive study, but we really want to closely look at Jesus, the leader of the church, the example he set, and the Word that he left for us. I would encourage you to continue this study on your own, using nothing but a good translation of God's Word to see just how specific Jesus was in his teaching his initial twelve disciples, eleven who later became apostles.

Now let's look at Jesus, the leader, and how he did things. Jesus did not always do things the same way all the time and that's an excellent example for leaders of the church today whether they are elders, preachers, deacons, or ministry leaders. He did things dependent on the situation. Today we call that situational leadership. For instance, when asked a question, Jesus responded to the questioner in different ways. Sometimes he responded to a question by asking a question. In the beginning of Matthew 15, the scribes and Pharisees were questioning Jesus and trying to trap him as they asked him about his disciples not washing their hands before they ate bread. Jesus responded with a question because he wanted the questioners to examine themselves because they were living by tradition or the letter of the law instead of by the commandments of God. Aren't some of us guilty of that today? We want to hold others to our traditions without really examining the Scriptures to see whether those traditions are according to God's Word.

In the next example, Jesus answered the question with a question and then he answered the follow-up question by illustrating the answer with a parable. Let's look at Luke 10:25-37. The lawyer first tried to trick Jesus by asking, "Teacher, what shall I do to inherit eternal life?" Jesus responded to the lawyer's question with this question, "What is written in the law? What is your reading [or understanding] of it?" This lawyer had a true understanding of the law and responded correctly to Jesus' question. "You shall love the Lord your God with all your heart, with all your soul, with all your strength, and with all your mind, and your neighbor as yourself."

When Jesus told him he had correctly answered the question, the lawyer then said, "And who is my neighbor?" Jesus then related the parable we commonly call the Parable of the Good Samaritan to the lawyer and then asked the lawyer which of the three in the parable was the neighbor. Again the lawyer answered correctly, "He who showed mercy on him." and Jesus then told the lawyer to go and do likewise. This was a true teaching moment and a great example for today's church leaders to do the same. When an occasion arises in today's church of the Lord that someone needs teaching, the elders, preacher, teacher, or some other ministry leaders should take the lead in teaching them. A teaching moment may never present itself again.

The third example I want to use we find in Matthew 21:18-22 when Jesus caused the non-fruit bearing fig tree to whither. His disciples asked why he had caused the tree to wither away so quickly. Jesus simply answered the question but in a way that he could use his answer to teach his disciples. It simply was not bearing fruit and that was why it was destroyed. Do we bear fruit for the kingdom? If not, are we in danger of being destroyed?

In these first two aforementioned examples, Jesus knows the answer lies within the Scriptures so Jesus questions the questioner by posing questions that will cause the questioner to look within the scriptural teachings for an answer and think on it while in the third example, he simply teaches his disciples that they need to be fruitful as Christians need to be fruitful in today's various congregations of the church of Christ. These are excellent examples of situational leadership. Jesus responded to questions based on the situation and used the opportunity to teach his followers or his potential followers who might be listening.

Jesus also wants leaders as well as all followers to be persistent and press on to accomplish whatever goals the individual sets for himself or herself or the congregation sets for itself. In Luke 11: 5-10, Jesus uses a parable of the need for loaves to feed visitors to teach this very important point. Jesus sums up the point in verses nine and ten with these words. "So I say to you, ask, and it will be given to you; seek, and you will find; knock, and it will be opened to you. For everyone who asks receives, and he who seeks finds, and to him who knocks it will be opened." Today's leaders in the church need to be teaching this lesson of persistence to their congregations in any ministry that the congregation decides to undertake.

Persistency or consistency in leaders is certainly an admirable and desired attribute or characteristic. Kouzes and Posner (2002) have studied leadership in many settings and found consistency between words and action to be vital to the success of the organization. Jim Collins (2001) writes that consistency is important to move from being a good organization to becoming a great organization. People look for leaders to do what they say they are going to do and also to do themselves the same things they ask their followers to do within the organization. Modern scholars and organizations can learn much about leadership by studying the Scriptures, and they might be surprised to find that modern man for all his wisdom is simply rediscovering what the greatest of teachers taught.

Jesus also taught this lesson of persistence in Luke 18:1-8 and this inspired writer, the physician Luke, leads into this parable of the widow and the judge with these words, "that men always ought to pray and not lose heart" (v. 1). The judge finally relents after the widow kept coming and asking for justice from her adversary. Persistence paid off then and persistence will pay off now.

A personal friend long ago reminded me of that lesson when I had a conversation with him about pursuing my doctorate degree. I was in my mid-fifties at the time and was looking to prolong my usefulness after I retired from my job in the telecommunications industry. I was considering how to prepare myself to teach at the college or university level. I had some reluctance because I was not sure I could manage the study load and continue to work full time for a few more years. He told me that I just needed to be persistent and that I could make it happen. He was right; I had forgotten God's lesson to "knock, and it will be opened to you." I received my doctorate in 2003 and I've been teaching since then, and I try every day to instill that lesson of persistence in my students both in the classroom and when speaking to the congregation where I worship, teach, or occasionally preach. Persistence is also a powerful lesson for those in the church who want to work to bring others to an understanding of the gospel and to have faith in Jesus so that they might do the things that the Scriptures tell one to do to become a Christian.

Jesus was also the greatest of communicators. This leadership trait is best described in Luke 24:32 after Jesus had appeared to his disciples. "And they said to one another, 'Did not our heart burn within us while He talked with us on the road, and while He opened the scriptures to us.'" Can you imagine someone who is so great a communicator that their words actually burn within you? Can you imagine the understanding of the Scriptures they must have had after this event? This is an excellent example of the charisma that Jesus demonstrated as a leader to his followers.

That passage of Scripture we commonly refer to as The Sermon on the Mount (Matthew 5-7) is also a great example of a great communicator. Jesus covers a broad spectrum of issues and teachings to the multitude that had gathered to hear him with instructions of how they could be complete or what God wanted them to be.

Jesus was also a great communicator without using words. Look at John 8:1-11. Again, the scribes and Pharisees are testing Jesus. Jesus just merely stooped down and wrote on the ground. When they persisted, he rose up and simply told them "He who is without sin among you, let him throw a stone at her first." He then resumed his writing on the ground. They got the message from the great communicator's actions!

The Scriptures contain many excellent examples of Jesus' ability to communicate. Look them up. Study them with the perspective of a great leader communicating to his followers because that is what Jesus did while he was here on the earth and it is what he continues to do through his Word. This is a tremendous example for all of us in the church. Communication solves problems and lack of communication weakens an organization. Many of the complaints that are heard from members of most congregations are that the leaders do not communicate effectively to the congregation. With all the technology that is available today, you would think that effective communication would not be the issue it is in many congregations.

Jesus is the Head of the church and as its leader was very fruitful in bringing followers to himself. He also expects his followers to be fruitful and productive (John 15:1-2). He set the example for us of honoring his Father and he expects us not only to honor him with our lips but also to honor him with our hearts (Matthew 15:8).

I want to leave you with this question for your personal reflection: Do you listen to God's Word to develop your leadership skills or do you bring lessons into the church from your worldly experience?

Today, many leaders in the various leadership roles of the church bring their worldly experience and skills into the church instead of looking to the Scriptures for the lessons taught there. I personally think that *all* followers of Christ are supposed to be leaders because he spent three years training his leadership team, the apostles. He then instructed them to "Go therefore and make disciples of all the nations, baptizing them in the name of the Father and of the Son and of the Holy Spirit, teaching them to observe all things that I have commanded you; and lo, I am with you always, *even* to the end of the age" (Matthew 28:18-19). I think there needs to be a stronger emphasis on "teaching them to observe all things that I have commended you." He wants all of us to be leaders in leading or bringing others to Christ. I would like to encourage you to continue this study on your own and look at Jesus not only as our Savior, but also to look at him as the leader who wants his followers to also be leaders.

Additional Study of the Head of the Church

- Jesus is the high priest of the church of Christ (Hebrews 5) and the believers and followers of Jesus are a kingdom of priests (I Peter 2:5-9).
- Matthew 23:9 "Do not call anyone on earth your father; for One is your Father, He who is in heaven."
- As we read the gospels we note a leadership characteristic of Jesus—he taught by conversations with his disciples, not necessarily at specific events but between events. An example—Matthew 13:3ff.
- Deuteronomy 6:4-9 conversations are opportunities to teach.
- We are surrounded by people but we live in isolation for the most part. We need to meet and engage people around us in conversation in order to "lead" them to Christ. All Christians should develop the "leadership" traits or characteristics that Jesus employed with those around him.
- We are creatures of habit and we deplore change. Look at the children of Israel. They complained and even wanted to return to Egypt instead of moving to a new life of freedom (Numbers 14:3-4). They were comfortable with slavery and wanted to return to that status quo. They were afraid of the uncertain future even though God said he would be with them.
- Jesus went straight to the source of a problem (Mark 4: 35-41).
- Jesus prayed for unity of his believers (Matt 18:19-20).
- Jesus' authority – Mark 1:21-28; John 17:2-3.
- God desires that all would be saved (I Timothy 2:3-4).
- Jesus is the same yesterday, today, and forever (Heb. 13:8).
- Communication by a leader – Jesus begins to tell his disciples of his death in Matthew 16 and then continues to communicate this with greater detail until his death.
- Christ as temple – John 1:14; John 2: 19-21; Mark 14:58; Acts 7:48; II Corinthians 5:1, 6:16; Ephesians 2;21-22; Hebrews 3:6-9, 9:11, 24.
- Christ as priest – Hebrews 4:14, 5:5-6, 10, 8:1.
- Examine the leadership lessons in Matthew 14:22-33.

Chapter 5
Authority, Vision, and Mission

"I am the Alpha and the Omega, the Beginning and the End," says the Lord, "who is and who was and who is to come, the Almighty" (Revelation 1:8).

Authority

The first thing one does when looking at the vision and mission of a group, organization, or institution is to look at the authority that brought the vision and mission into being. The vision and mission should be provided by the head of the organization, or in our case, the organism and to do so that person or group of persons must have some authority. Since we have already examined the head of the organism, and determined it to be Jesus Christ, we will now look at his authority from a scriptural perspective. The following definition of authority is from Holman's Bible Dictionary:

> "*Authority* in biblical usage, describes the absolute power and freedom of God, and claims that He is the source of all other authorization or power." (Denison, 2004)

Authority, in a religious context, is not often used in the Old Testament of the Bible and examining the Old Testament context of authority is not important in this particular study; therefore, we will not go into a discussion of Old Testament usage of the term. In the New Testament, "the Greek word commonly translated authority is *exousia* and is used to denote freedom, choice, right, ruling, or official power" (Fair, 1996, p. 311). *Exousia* is used in various contexts in the New Testament. It can mean the ruling power of government officials as used in Romans 13:1. In a general sense, it can mean the power or right to do something as it is used in John 12:1. It can also be used to denote the sense of freedom to make choices (I Corinthians 9:12).

In the religious context in the New Testament, *exousia* is used:

- to denote that the authority of God is axiomatic (a self evident truth) and absolute (Revelation 1:8).
- to denote the authority granted by the Father to Jesus (Matthew 28:18; John 17:1,2) who will judge the world (Acts 17:30,31).
- to denote the authority of the Holy Spirit and God's Word (John 14:16-17).
- as the authority granted to the apostles by Jesus (II Corinthians 10:8; 13:10).

From these Scriptures, we find that *exousia* denotes absolute authority in matters of Christian religion and is reserved for God, Christ, the apostles, and the inspired Scriptures. Scripturally, this authority does not reside in the church of Christ or any person in the church of Christ.

James C. Denison, a contributor to Holman's Bible Dictionary, gives a history of the use of authority in the church in that document. The meaning of authority has undergone interpretation changes. Early church leaders were in agreement that the Bible was the primary source of authority but soon began using authority based on tradition and that "tradition authority" was viewed as equal to "Bible authority" by the fourth century in the evolved Roman Catholic Church. There were efforts made during the Reformation to go back to the Scriptures for authority but tradition was still an influence. The Anabaptists and early Baptists looked to the Bible for authority as a foundational framework for their theological beliefs and maintained that all church doctrine should be derived from and consistent with the Bible itself. Yet, they write constitutions and conventions that adhere more to their tradition. The Roman Catholic Church made some attempts to increase its emphasis on the church and authority by its affirmation of papal infallibility pertaining to faith and its practice in 1870. Then in 1962-65, Vatican II balanced papal authority with that of bishops and "interpreted both authorities in a ministerial context" (Dennison, 2004).

Liberal Protestantism located authority in man's reason and experience in the nineteenth century about the time that the Restoration Movement declared that all legitimate authority comes directly from God or indirectly from God through his Son, Jesus Christ. However, traditionalism crept into the Restoration Movement because of the influence of the early restoration's influence from the protestant communities from which restoration began. In the organization of the modern world, authority is gained in a variety of ways: position in an organization, granted to one person by another person (empowerment), or assumed by a person who steps up and takes charge (emergent or authentic leadership). The same or similar uses are found in the New Testament: power of government officials (Luke 19:17; 20:20; John 19:10; Revelation 17:12); used in the general sense of power or right to do something (Luke 12:5; John 1:12; Acts 8:19); and used in references to the sense of freedom to make choices (I Corinthians 9:12; II Thessalonians 3:9). These are not the uses of authority we want to make the reader cognitive of.

An example of the authority we want you to understand is the authority of Jesus. Jesus tells his apostles that he has authority in Matthew 28:18. "And Jesus came and spoke to them saying, "All authority has been given to me in heaven and on earth." God granted absolute authority to his Son Jesus (Matthew 28:18; John 17:2) and through that authority, he will judge the world (Acts 17:30, 31).

I don't think that we need to go further with Jesus' authority because all Christians certainly recognize that he does have authority from his Father. We need to go forward with looking at how that authority should influence the mission and vision of the congregations of the Lord during the first century of its existence and down to the autonomous congregation level. If we abide by the structure of the church in the New Testament, we have no need of the hierarchical structure we see in Christian religious groups today. Leadership is responsible for the mission and vision of an organization or group that falls in the shadow of the leader. That leadership in the church should be Jesus Christ and he set the vision and mission.

Mission and Vision

"A mission statement describes the long-term purpose of the organization [organism] …" (Cummings & Worley, 2005). A mission statement is a viable part of any group's, institution's, or organization's strategic plan and is set by the respective leader and/or leadership team. Since we recognize that the elders of a church of Christ are the spiritual leaders of the group (discussed in a later chapter), they are and should be instrumental in formulating a mission and vision for the local congregation of the Lord and communicating that vision and mission to the membership based on input from the congregation about the various ministries the congregants would like to be involved with. The congregational vision and mission should be linked to that vision and mission set by Jesus. It should be communicated often to the congregants.

Jesus introduced the mission of the church in Matthew 28:18-20.

> "And Jesus came and spoke to them saying, "All authority has been given to me in heaven and on earth. Go therefore and make disciples of all nations, baptizing them in the name of the Father and of the Son and of the Holy Spirit, teaching them to observe all things that I have commanded you; and lo, I am with you always, *even* to the end of the age." (Matthew 28:18-20)

God formatted the mission statement, the guiding principle of the church, and his Son delivered it to the world. Jesus also emphasizes his authority when he delivered the mission statement to his apostles.

Examine what is being said in this mission statement. Not only are we to make disciples of all nations, we are to baptize them in the name of the Father and of the Son and of the Holy Spirit, we are to teach them all things that Jesus commanded, and he will be with us always. This is a very simple, easy to understand mission statement. Are we doing all we can do as a congregation to carry out this mission? How are we going to teach if we do not study God's Word, the Bible, so that we can be teaching all things that Jesus commanded us?

Do you remember the illustration of the vine that Christ relates to his disciples in John 15:1-8? He tells us that if we do not bear fruit we will be cut off. If we bear fruit we will be pruned to bear even more fruit. He concludes this passage with, "If you keep My commandants, you will abide in My love, just as I have kept My Father's commandants and abide in his love. These things I have spoken to you, that My joy may remain in you, and that your joy may be full" (verses 9-11). He is doing what any good leader would do in that he's re-emphasizing the need to follow his commandments that the disciples have received in the past, have received in the present, and will receive in the future. That's why it's important for a local congregation to have its own mission statement and that the mission statement is linked to the mission statement given to the Lord's church by the head of the church, Jesus Christ. When the leadership of a congregation adopts a strong mission statement and provides a strong vision to the congregation, and the congregation makes sure all its ministries are linked to the mission of the church of Christ in some fashion, then exponential growth will occur in the Lord's church (See the early chapters of Acts).

Jesus had his own mission statement. In his prayers as recorded in John 17 we get a glimpse of his true mission—to glorify God, to give eternal life to his followers, and to do the will of his Father. He glorified God and finished the work here on earth that he was given to do. He manifested God's name to his followers and gave them the words that God had given him. He also stated that he sent them into the world so that others would believe in him. Jesus' mission was multi-pronged. He earlier explained to his disciples that he would die and that in dying he would bring increase as a grain of wheat does when it falls to the earth and dies. He told them that his purpose was to die (John 12:23-27). Jesus told his disciples that he was returning to Heaven after his crucifixion and resurrection to prepare a place for those who believe in him and he said he would come again to receive those believers (John 14:1-4). He also told them that he had another purpose and that was to prepare a place in heaven for his believers and that he would come again for them (John 14:1-4). In this passage, he was also encouraging his followers—another mark of an excellent leader.

Jesus also had a vision. It is described by Paul as that day when he will deliver the kingdom or church to God the Father (I Corinthians 15:24). In modern leadership, organizational, or business training, a vision is a concept of where the leader wants the group, organization, or institution to be in the future. You first examine where you currently are, present state, and then visualize where you and/or the group to be in the future, future state. In other words, what will the ministry, the congregation, and each individual look like in its new envisioned place? Then each ministry must plan how it is going to move from its present state to that envisioned future state and this is called the transitional state. The transitional state relates to the various ministries in which a congregation may involve itself.

This study is not about bringing change into the scriptural aspects of the church but to encourage all those who identify themselves as Christian to bring about change in their level of commitment to the choice they've made to serve our Lord and Savior, Jesus Christ. Each of us needs to examine where we are involved or not involved in the work of the congregation and make whatever changes we need to make to carry out the mission of the church as long as those changes are in accordance with the Scriptures and under the spiritual guidance of the congregational leaders.

Just as Jesus had a mission or purpose, the Holy Spirit also has a mission revealed in John 16. He was foretold by Jesus to the apostles as another Helper that would remain with them forever (John 14:13). Jesus had to leave this world before the Helper could come (John 16:7). Jesus told the apostles that when the Helper comes his mission would be to convict the world of sin and righteousness and judgment (John 16:8-11). Second, he will speak as he has been authorized to speak. That authority comes from God. The Holy Spirit also speaks and guides the believers in Christ (John 8:13) through the inspired Word of God. And finally, he glorifies Christ and declares the Word to believers (John 8:14-15) through their study of God's Word. The Holy Spirit's mission is linked to that of Jesus' mission to establish the church.

You might say, "All of this is well and good but what has it got to do with me as an individual?" Each of us should have a mission statement and a plan to carry it out just as we read about the apostle Paul in Ephesians. Paul was engaged in the work of the church and in explaining himself to the church at Ephesus, he revealed his mission. Let's look at the passage of Scripture in Ephesians 3:8-12.

> To me, who am less than the least of all the saints, this grace was given, that I should preach among the Gentiles the unsearchable riches of Christ, and to make all see what *is* the fellowship of the mystery, which from the beginning of the ages has been hidden in God who created all things through Jesus Christ; to the intent that now the manifold wisdom of God might be made known by the church to the principalities and powers in the heavenly *places,* according to the eternal purpose which He accomplished in Christ Jesus our Lord, in whom we have boldness and access with confidence through faith in Him.

Paul saw his primary mission to teach and preach among the Gentiles that the manifold wisdom of God be made known to them. There needs to be emphasis on "that the manifold wisdom of God be made known by the church." Paul would not be here forever. We will not be here forever. We need to develop our spiritual gifts to be as productive as possible while we are here so that others will have a church as much like the church of Christ described in the Bible as possible.

A good statement of Paul's vision is found in Philippians 3:16 where he states, "Nevertheless, to *the degree* that we have already attained, let us walk by the same rule, let us be of the same mind." This vision is linked to Jesus' prayer for unity that we find in John 17:21-22. Without unity of the mind and of the rule, the church is in chaos and without God's truth. Paul's examples are excellent examples for each Christian—we should individually develop our mission and vision, ascertaining that they are consistent with God's inspired Word and in accordance with the mission and vision of the local congregation as established by its spiritual leaders and linked to the Great Commission.

Now that we've discussed the mission and vision of Jesus, the Holy Spirit, and the apostle Paul, let's look at the mission and vision of the church of Christ from a universal perspective.

The mission of the Lord's church is found as a commandant in Matthew 28:18-20 as previously noted. Jesus said:

> All authority has been given to Me in heaven and on earth. Go therefore and make disciples of all nations, baptizing them in the name of the Father, and of the Son and of the Holy Spirit, teaching them to observe all things that I have commanded you; and lo, I am with you always, *even* to the end of the age. Amen.

This is a very simple statement as every group's, institution's, or organization's mission statements should be. It is a commandment by Jesus Christ himself. It says, "Go therefore and make disciples of all nations." This does not exclude any person, anywhere, anytime. It says that those who go should go "teaching them to observe all things that I have commanded you." Jesus spent three years selecting and teaching his disciples. Jesus taught his disciples to be teachers, he taught them to be ministers, he taught them to be preachers, and most of all he taught them to be involved. He also taught them many other things. He did not teach them that all they had to do was accept his salvation and then do nothing. He did not teach them that all they had to do was to have faith.

The church of Christ also has a mission (Matthew 28:18-20) and a purpose and that purpose is that "the manifold wisdom of God might be made known by the church" (Ephesians 3:10) and that purpose or mission is also to be linked to Jesus' mission or the great commission that he left for us. Autonomous congregations of the Lord might elect to go about doing the work of the church in different ways and that's why it's important to have a congregation mission statement. That mission statement does not have to be elaborate or all encompassing but just something to rally the congregation around. Everyone can't be involved in all things nor can congregations be necessarily involved in every area needing ministry. The larger a congregation is, the more resources it has, and the better equipped it is to participate in many different ministries.

God formatted the mission statement to the church of Christ, the guiding principle of the church, and his Son delivered it to the world. Each autonomous congregation should develop its own mission statement and make sure that it's linked to the original mission statement, the Great Commission. If all members are committed to doing the work of the church, the mission statement will help the congregation remain focused and help them to become more unified. Unity is a major problem in many of today's Christian groups.

Again, let's review the mission statement of this organization, the church of Christ:

> And Jesus came and spoke to them saying, "All authority has been given to me in heaven and on earth. Go therefore and make disciples of all nations, baptizing them in the name of the Father and of the Son and of the Holy Spirit, teaching them to observe all things that I have commanded you; and lo, I am with you always, *even* to the end of the age (Matthew 28: 18-20).

Examine what is being said in this mission statement. First, all authority has been given to the Son by the Father. Next, Christians are to go and make disciples of all nations. Those who become disciples are to be baptized in the name of the Father and of the Son and of the Holy Spirit. Those who evangelize are to teach the new disciples all things that Jesus commanded the apostles (they are the ones who received the original mission statement or commandment), and he will be with us always. How are we going to all of these things in this mission statement if we do not study God's Word, the Bible, so that we can be teaching all things that Jesus commands us through his everlasting word?

Paul understood that he was to teach others (Acts 19:8-10) so by deduction we can know that those who were taught, taught others as was first told by Jesus to the apostles when he gave them, and by extrapolation, all Christians, what we know as the Great Commission.

Mission statements are usually accompanied with a vision statement and our vision as Christians is to gain entry into heaven. Simply put, the vision of the church is for its members to gain an eternal home in heaven. John gives us a picture of heaven in Revelation 21:1-8. In heaven we will not suffer from death, there will be no sorrow, no crying, and no pain.

The gospel was taught to the entire world during the time of the first century church (Colossians 1:23) and we should be doing the same thing today. They did it by daily teaching and preaching and they did not cease (Acts 5:42). The apostles told the congregation in Jerusalem to pick out deacons to do the work of the church so that they, the Apostles, could remain focused on the spiritual aspects of growing the church. They continued to teach and preach and the Word of God spread (Acts 6:7). The very purpose of the church is to bring glory to God through Jesus Christ (Ephesians 1:11, 12; 3:20-21) and focusing on the mission of the church of Christ will help each of us to accomplish this.

I once saw this on the sign in front of a building used for worship purposes: "God promised to feed the sparrows but he did not promise to throw it into the nest." This is plain common sense when we explore the Scriptures and see what God intended the church to accomplish—"Go into all the world." When we put on Christ, we put on a new creature (Colossians 3). We are required to do something; we are required to take action, just like the sparrows do to gather the food that God supplies.

Every congregation that seeks to worship and be structured according to the Scriptures should have a mission statement, whether it is the great commission or some other words that are linked to the great commission. I have observed some very good congregational mission statements over the years and the leadership of congregations that attempt to worship and be structured along the New Testament instructions are responsible to provide that mission statement to their congregation and keep it ever present in their sight. That is just one thing that brings congregations into unity and alignment with God's instructions for the church.

Jesus provides the vision for the church—everlasting life in heaven. Church leaders and ministry leaders must provide mini-visions that link their respective congregations and ministries to Jesus' vision. Each individual in the congregation, whether they be ministers, elders, deacons, evangelists, teachers, or just "plain members" should have a mission statement and it should be written in their mind and on their heart. All of us have a function in the organism known as the church of Christ.

Additional Study about Authority

In the realm of religion there is scriptural authority. In the New Testament we find authority (exousia) used in a variety of ways.

- Power of government officials (Luke 19:17; 20:20; John 19:10; Revelation 17:12)
- Used in the general sense of power or right to do something (Luke 12:5; John 1:12; Acts 8:19)
- Used in references to the sense of freedom to make choices (I Corinthians 9:12; II Thessalonians 3:9).
- God granted absolute authority to his Son Jesus (Matthew 28:18; John 17:2) and through that authority, he will judge the world (Acts 17: 30, 31).

Chapter 6
The Work of the New Testament Church

"And daily in the temple, and in every house, they did not cease teaching and preaching Jesus as the Christ" (Acts 5:42).

Have you considered the divisions of labor in the church? There are those in the church who have specific functional roles such as deacons and elders and we will discuss those functional roles in other chapters of this work. And there is work that all Christians are to do according to their abilities! All members of the church are supposed to be evangelistic in some way; we are to edify one another in some way; and we are to be benevolent in some way. When we examine the first century church of Christ, there was work that was accomplished by the congregation. This division of labor was based on talents or spiritual gifts that they had been given by God (Romans 12:3-8; I Corinthians 12:1-10; Ephesians 4:11-12; I Peter 4: 10-11). And we also know from the teachings of Jesus himself, that those talents could and should be increased by the practice and exercise of those gifts (Matthew 25:14-30). We find that Jesus brought a new covenant and those Christians fulfilled that new covenant with love and service for each other and their neighbors (Galatians 5:13-14; Romans 13:8).

Again, using the Greek word *ekklesia* or those "called out" combined with two other Greek words *Koinonia*—meaning communion, creates a relationship of Christ and the believer and of the believers with one another in a partnership or unity—and *Agape meaning* "dearness," "affection," "high regard," or "love", I come up with this definition of the *church*: That body of believers who are called out into a unified, loving, covenant relationship with Jesus and with each other. As such, that body of believers should be involved with evangelism, edification, and benevolence in whatever ministry they decide to work as a fit for their respective talents or skills.

Jesus lifted up his eyes to heaven and said to his Father, "I have glorified You on the earth. I have finished the work which You have given me to do" (John 17:4). If Jesus recognized that he needed to work here on earth, don't you think that all Christians need to be involved in the work of the church of Christ? Paul certainly was and was not afraid to announce it whenever the opportunity presented itself.

When the inspired writer, Luke, told of Paul's oration before King Agrippa, Paul stated how that new Christians, both Jew and Gentile "... should repent, turn to God, and do works befitting repentance" (Acts 26:20). Paul affirms Jesus' position about work, but there are some that would teach that all one has to do is have faith. The brother of Jesus was very simplistic about Christians doing work in his writings. He simply said, "Do you see that faith was working together with his works, and by works faith was made perfect" (James 2:22) in reference to the work of Abraham when he offered Isaac his son. Therefore all Christians are to be involved in the work of the church of Christ according to the talents they have been given.

Evangelism

One division of labor for members of the church is evangelism. Again we turn back to Paul's writings to the Ephesians, "And He Himself gave some *to be* apostles, some prophets, some evangelists, and some pastors and teachers, for the equipping of the saints for the work of ministry, for the edifying the body of Christ," (Ephesians 4:11-12). Those divisions of labor we see in the Scriptures are all contained here, preaching and evangelizing, equipping the saints (members) for various ministries, and edifying the church, the Body of Christ. The Great Commission is an actual commandment by Jesus Christ to evangelize the world.

> "And Jesus came and spoke to them, saying, "All authority has been given to Me in heaven and on earth. Go therefore and make disciples of all nations, baptizing them in the name of the Father, and of the Son and of the Holy Spirit, teaching them to observe all things that I have commanded you; and lo, I am with you always, *even* to the end of the age." Amen. (Matthew 28:18-20)

Matthew's writings are reinforced by Mark's account of the same commandant in Mark 16:15-16.

Christians are not only to evangelize or preach in the worship services but they are to go to the entire world teaching, evangelizing, and baptizing. Acts 5:42 reveals a glimpse of the first century members of the church and how they worked to sow the seeds so that God could provide the increase. "And daily in the temple, and in every house, they did not cease teaching and preaching Jesus *as* the Christ." The results of the efforts of these early Christians sowing the seed are that literally thousands came to know Christ as their Lord and Savior. That is apparently not the case in today's society. In a 2007 study, the Barna Group found a slight decrease in the number of adults proclaiming themselves as Christians and many fewer teens who claim Christianity as their religion. Similar numbers were found in an analysis of U.S. Census data by The Pew Forum on Religion and Life (United States Religious Demographic Profile, 2006). Then the question posited here is: "If the church of Christ grew at such astronomical numbers during the first century of its establishment, why is it not growing today?" The examination of the first century church suggests that the decrease in growth of the church today may be because Christians today are not as focused on the work of the church as they were in the first century. I would suggest that this may be because we have institutionalized the church and expect others to be responsible for church growth.

Paul charges Timothy concerning preaching the Word in II Timothy 4:1-2, "I charge *you* therefore before God and the Lord Jesus Christ, who will judge the living and the dead at his appearing and his kingdom: Preach the Word! Be ready in season and out of season. Convince, rebuke, exhort, with all longsuffering and teaching." The message that Paul is relaying to Timothy is relevant to all Christians. Members of the church should be ready at all times to teach and preach the gospel message of Christ. We should preach with conviction, rebuking those actions that are sin. We should build one another up and do it by teaching the things God's Word contains with patience. To accomplish this we need to build ourselves spiritually.

Peter tells us how Christians are to grow spiritually:

> But also for this very reason, giving all diligence, add to your faith virtue, to virtue knowledge, to knowledge self-control, to self-control perseverance, to perseverance godliness, to godliness brotherly kindness, and to brotherly kindness love. For if these things are yours and abound,

> *you will be* neither barren nor unfruitful in the knowledge of our Lord Jesus Christ. For he who lacks these things is shortsighted, even to blindness, and has forgotten that he was cleansed from his old sins. Therefore brethren, be even more diligent to make your call and election sure, for if you do these things you will never stumble; for so an entrance will be supplied to you abundantly into the everlasting kingdom of our Lord and Savior Jesus Christ. (II Peter 1:5-11)

Many today simply study this passage as Christian graces but I say to you that it is a formula of characteristics to grow and mature as the Christian starts with faith and adds the other Christian characteristics until they mature when they obtain agape love. Peter gives us not only a recipe for growth as a Christian but also assures us that if we do these things we can be sure of an entrance into Jesus' everlasting kingdom which is heaven. The church is temporary and will end when the earth is no more. Jesus will deliver the church to his Father so that the members of the Lord's church may spend eternity with our Heavenly Father. God, Jesus, the Holy Spirit, and heaven are eternal. If you lack these building blocks or Christian characteristics for spiritual growth, you will be shortsighted, blind, and will have forgotten your salvation.

Edification

The second division of labor of the church is edification of other Christians. Christians are to build up one another's faith. Why is edification or the building up of one's faith so important in the church? Luke writes of this in Acts 9:31. "Then the churches throughout all Judea, Galilee, and Samaria had peace and were edified. And walking in fear of the Lord and in the comfort of the Holy Spirit, they were multiplied." What do we read here? These churches were at peace, they were edified, and as they walked in reverent fear to God and in the comfort of the Holy Spirit they multiplied. See how the church can grow! One small passage here just tells so much about how Christians should behave and as a result of that correct behavior, the church will grow. Are we to be constantly bickering with one another? No, that impedes edification and subsequently growth—when we are at peace, the church grows. Are we to walk in the world? No, we are to walk in reverent fear to God and do his will, and his will is that we evangelize the world, and the church grows. Are Christians to be comfortable with the world and Satan? No, Christians are to be in comfort with the Holy Spirit and the church will grow.

We've already covered this verse but it need to be looked at again. "And He Himself gave some *to be* apostles, some prophets, some evangelists, and some pastors and teachers, for the equipping of the saints for the work of ministry, for the edifying the body of Christ," (Ephesians 4:11-12). One of the functions of evangelists, elders, and teachers is to equip the members or saints of their respective congregations to edify the church, the body of Christ. Elders are also known as pastors (Ephesians 4:11), shepherds (I Peter 5:2-4), rulers (Hebrews 13:17), and bishops or overseers (Acts 20:28; I Timothy 3:1-7). These terms all refer to the same persons but are applied to the church leaders depending on the function they are carrying out at a particular moment and we will discuss this further in the chapter on elders and their functional role or ministry in the church of the Lord.

We are told by Paul that "love edifies" (I Corinthians 8:1). This is that Christian characteristic we just discussed. False teachers can tear down edification by causing disputes in the church. Godly faith edifies the church (I Timothy 1:4). But there are those servants of the evil one who will test our faith and consequently try to tear down the church. Paul commands the church at Thessalonica to comfort and edify one another (I Thessalonians 5:11). The church is commanded to edify one another, and love and faith are aids or tools that help the Christians edify each other.

Jesus commanded his followers, his disciples to love one another.

> This is My commandment, that you love one another as I have loved you. Greater love has no one than this, than to lay down one's life for his friends. You are My friends if you do whatever I command you. No longer do I call you servants, for a servant does not know what his master is doing; but I have called you friends, for all things that I heard from My Father I have made known to you. You did not choose Me, but I chose you and appointed you that you should go and bear fruit, and *that* your fruit should remain, that whatever you ask the Father in My name He may give you. These things I command you, that you love one another. (John 15:12-17)

Why do you think he commanded us to love one another? It's very obvious—love of another builds that person up and at the same time it builds you up. That's what Christian love, agape love, is about. It is the most important characteristic that a Christian can develop. Without agape love, Christians are nothing.

The public or corporate worship service is not only when a congregation of the Lord comes together to worship the one and true God, but is another time of edification. Paul wrote to the Corinthian church, "How is it then, brethren? Whenever you come together, each of you has a psalm, has a teaching, has a tongue, has a revelation. Let all things be done for edification" (I Corinthians 14:26). The worship service is a time for edification by singing and by teaching. Christians are to "pursue the things *which make* for peace and the things by which one may edify another" (Romans 14:19). Christians do not assemble together to be entertained, they assemble together to worship God and to edify each other so that the church will grow.

Christians can edify themselves through God's Word. Edification of your self can be accomplished by the study of God's Word. Listen to the words of Paul as recorded by Luke in Acts 20:32. "So now, brethren, I commend you to God and to the word of His grace, which is able to build you up and give you an inheritance among all those who are sanctified." The Word of God builds us up, edifies us, and it also, as a bonus, gives us an inheritance with other Christians in heaven. God's Word is powerful. We need to study it every day—not just read it but study it.

Our ministers, preachers, elders, deacons, teachers, and every member need to heed the words of Paul as he addresses the sins of the Corinthians. "Again, do you think that we excuse ourselves to you? We speak before God in Christ. But *we do* all things, beloved, for your edification" (II Corinthians 12:19). If the preaching or the teaching or the reading of the Scriptures edifies us we will be more able to resist the sins of the world. We are all in this game together as Christians. We need to help each other gain entrance to heaven. We need not forget someone that has become a Christian and we think he or she is now safe because that person can also fall back into the wiles of Satan. There are those that say that once a person is saved he is always saved but God's inspired writer Peter tells us that this is simply not true. In the second chapter of II Peter, he warns of those false teachers who will come into the church and they will entice us with deceptive words. Some of us who escape the lusts of the world will again become entangled in those lusts for worldly things. Peter says this of those who fall away in such a manner.

> For if, after they have escaped the pollutions of the world through the knowledge of the Lord and Savior Jesus

> Christ, they are again entangled in them and overcome, the latter end is worse for them than the beginning. For it would have been better for them not to have known the way of righteousness, than having known *it,* to turn from the holy commandment delivered to them. But it has happened to them according to the true proverb: *"A dog returns to his own vomit,"* and, "a sow, having washed, to her wallowing in the mire." (II Peter 2: 20-22)

Are you in danger of returning to your own filth of whatever lust beckons to you? We are all engaged in a battle with Satan and it is only through God's Word that we can fend him off. In a small survey of Christians that I conducted as partial preparation for this book, when asked to identify the major problems facing the church today, the second most frequent problem identified was the loss of newly baptized Christians. The first major problem identified in that survey was the loss of our very own children from Christian families. And the third most serious problem facing the church was poor or ineffective leadership. Again, based on interviews with ministers, elders, and members of Christian religious groups, the failure of leadership in the church was a result of the institutionalization of the church as opposed to viewing the church as an organism and their role as one serving through leadership. The church has become so institutionalized, or rigidly organized, that members rely on those they have hired or selected to lead them to do everything in the work of the church while they attend when it is convenient and don't get any deeper involved than simply attending the worship services. Being a Christian is not a spectator sport; it is a personal commitment!

Benevolence

The third division of labor in the congregations of the church of the Lord is benevolence. Christians are to be benevolent especially to other Christians (Galatians 6:10). The first Christians called to attend to the benevolent needs of the widows in the church are also generally referred to as deacons in the first century church albeit the Scriptures never refer to them specifically as deacons. Some of the Hellenistic widows were being neglected in their needs. Seven men of good reputation, full of the Holy Spirit and wisdom, were appointed to carry out the work of ministering to the widows so the apostles could continue in the spiritual work of the church (Acts 6:1-6). We will find that same structure in any congregation of the Lord that elects to follow the pattern of the New Testament church today; elders carry out the spiritual care of the Word and of the congregation and deacons or other ministry leaders carry out the ministries that a congregation decides it needs to serve the congregation and the community in which it resides.

James tells us that "Pure and undefiled religion before God and the Father is this; to visit orphans and widows in their trouble, *and* to keep oneself unspotted from the world" (James 1:27). This does not cover all the benevolent work that could and should be shown by Christians to the world but is the very basic level of benevolence in which the church should be involved. If we just do this we will be undefiled as long as we stay away from the ways of the world.

Paul tells us in the Galatian letter that we should remember the poor (Galatians 2:10). Also, remember what Paul wrote to the Galatians in 6:10, "Therefore, as we have opportunity, let us do good to all, especially to those who are of the household of faith." The term "household of faith" describes the members of the Lord's church. We are to pay particular attention to the members of the church. We sometimes forget those in our fellowship; maybe it's because we're too close to them, but they might need assistance just as any other person who is outside the faith needs help.

I'd like to close this section on benevolence by reminding you of the parable of the Good Samaritan. When Jesus used this parable to teach his disciples, he knew how much the Jews despised the Samaritans so he used this teaching story to really get their attention. It simply answers the question, who is our real neighbor? Our neighbors are any folk that we come in contact with wherever and whenever. If we take every opportunity to serve others, we will grow spiritually and the church will grow numerically.

Chapter 7
Church Culture

"So continuing daily with one accord in the temple, and breaking bread from house to house, they ate their food with gladness and simplicity of heart, praising God and having favor with all the people. And the Lord added to the church daily those who were being saved"
(Acts 2:46-47).

When we visit a group, organization, or institution we notice certain things about it that inform us about it. What we are observing is the culture of the group, organization, or institution. Schein (1992) defines group culture as:

> A pattern of shared basic assumptions that the group learned as it solved its problems of external adaption and internal integration, that has worked well enough to be considered valid and, therefore, to be taught to new members as the correct way to perceive, think, and feel in relation to those problems. (p. 12)

In the study of organizational culture there are three levels of culture. The first level is labeled *Artifacts* and is those visible organizational structures and processes that we notice; we see them, we feel them, and we hear them. In other words, "The way things are done around here." These artifacts can be hard to decipher until you're comfortable with the organization and they become more self-evident; however, artifacts are clearly visible. They are the way in which the group behaves. In a congregation's building these would be bulletin boards, wall hangings, and so forth.

The second level of culture is the *Espoused Values*. These espoused values are found in the strategies, goals, and philosophies of the group. They are those things that justify the existence of the organization. Espoused values are not necessarily visible to a casual visitor to the group and can only be understood by digging into the documented mission statement and strategy of the group and determining whether the organization is fulfilling that mission statement and its strategy. In the scriptural church, certainly the espoused values would be from God's Word. But what if the congregation has strayed from God's Word? This has happened to many Christian groups over time and so this study is about truing up the compass and getting a congregation back on track if the congregation's leaders feel it is necessary.

The third level of culture is the *Basic Underlying Assumptions* and they are the unconscious, taken for granted beliefs, perceptions, thoughts, and feelings of the group. It is from these basic underlying assumptions that the group derives its values and actions. There are interactions between all three levels of culture. There may be strategies and philosophies in place, but if they are not clearly understood by the group, basic underlying assumptions become the de facto standard. You may also look at these as "traditions."

We as humans need cognitive stability; therefore, it is difficult to change the culture of a group, organization, or institution. If what is proposed by a leader is effective and continues to be effective, then his or her assumption comes to be the shared basic assumption of the group. Jesus and his apostles had a basic assumption about the church but over time, man has influenced that founding assumption and gradually changed the shared basic assumption into the many Christian religious groups we see around us.

If we go back to the Scriptures and examine the way that the first century church behaved, we can determine its basic shared assumption. If we then compare that behavior to a congregation's behavior today and determine that there is a difference and the congregation wants to truly conduct itself according to the Scriptures, then the leadership of the congregation has to lead that effort. This change back to the original intent of the church will be time-consuming, difficult, and will cause anxiety; therefore, there will be resistance because the human being likes stability and resists change even when it is good for him.

The congregational leaders have to decide what the current state of the congregation is, and have to devise and oversee a transition to the desired state of the congregation as it is depicted in God's Word.

As followers of Christ and members of a congregation of the Lord's church we have to be obedient to those that lead us (I Thessalonians 5:12, 13; I Timothy 5:17; Hebrews 13:7, 17) as long as they lead according to the scriptural guidelines that the first century church established. By examining the culture of a congregation, the elders or shepherds of the congregation can measure its behavior against the Scriptures it is supposed to be using as a guideline. This should be an on-going process and implementing a day of prayer and planning periodically, or some similar process, is a great way to constantly monitor the congregation and its work so that if it drifts away from the mission it can be brought back to its original mission. This monitoring of the congregation should be conducted by its spiritual leaders, the elders, but it is also the responsibility of every member to monitor whether things are being done according to the inspired Word.

God told us through His prophet Ezekiel, "Say to them: '*As* I live,' says the Lord GOD, 'I have no pleasure in the death of the wicked, but that the wicked turn from his way and live. Turn, turn from your evil ways! For why should you die, O house of Israel?" (Ezekiel 35:11). It is God's desire that we all come to him, and that's why congregational planning is important. And that's why understanding the culture of today's autonomous congregations by their respective elders or shepherds, as well as other ministry leaders and the members themselves is important.

As we look at the first century church as recorded in the New Testament, we find several indicators of its culture. The saved continued steadfastly in the doctrine the apostles taught them, in fellowship with one another, in the breaking of bread, and in prayers. They were together and had all things in common, even selling their possessions to meet the needs of others (Acts 2: 42-45). These first century Christians were receiving instruction, they were observing the Lord's Supper, they were engaging in corporate prayer, and engaging in a very effective outreach effort. These early verses of Scripture disclose to us that these early Christians were enthusiastic about the gift of salvation they had received. I have visited congregations while traveling that causes me to wonder if they've ever heard the Word because they are so unenthusiastic in their services.

Many, if not all, of the early Christians exhibited a very strong work ethic and Paul shares that with us in Romans 16:1-4 when he acknowledges the work of Phoebe, Priscilla, and Aquila. They also exhibited and practiced hospitality as evident in the previously mentioned Scripture, Acts 2. That practice continued and one example by Paul was in the first Corinthian letter, "I am glad about the coming of Stephanas, Fortunatus, and Achaicus, for what was lacking on your part they supplied" (I Corinthians 16:17). Paul is also an example of how the early Christians continued to evangelize. "And he reasoned in the synagogue every Sabbath, and persuaded both Jews and Greeks" (Acts 18:4).

When we put these things together we see a culture of instruction and learning, of corporate prayer, of observing the Lord's Supper and baptism, of hospitality, of strong work ethic, of evangelism, and of brotherly love. I need to interject here that during the first century, Moffatt (1938) found that there were only two "sacraments" that were observed by the church of Christ—baptism and the Lord's Supper. Moffatt also describes the worship services as very primitive. There were lessons from the Word, prayer and "responsive Amens," praise to God with the recitation of psalms. As they became available, the epistles from the various New Testament writers were also read and discussed. Moffatt's words are similar to the description given to us in Ephesians, "speaking to one another in psalms and hymns and spiritual songs, singing and making melody in your heart to the Lord, giving thanks always for all things to God the Father in the name of our Lord Jesus Christ, submitting to one another in the fear of God" (Ephesians 5:19-21). The indication is that the worship service should be simple and that all members need to be involved in the worship; we should not be there to be entertained but to worship God and share in edifying each other.

A strong indicator of the culture of an organization is how it makes decisions. Decision making has a great influence on the behavior of the group. This is important to understand because when people feel that they are a part of the group's culture and that their voice matters, they will do more for the group. There are three situations in the New Testament where the decision making process of the church was revealed. There is not a single situation recorded where a board of elders or other leaders made decisions acting independently on behalf of the church. As the church has been institutionalized over the centuries, beginning about the end of the first century, Christians began to forfeit their responsibility in making their own decisions concerning how they would serve the Lord and giving that function to those that were over them.

A hierarchy began to develop and it told Christians to follow the edicts of the leadership. Today we see little involvement in the congregation's work as well as a lack of support of ministries in the church by many members. Based on what I have read and studied and learned through talking to church leaders, preachers, and church members, I believe that lack of involvement and support is because members do not feel they are a part of the work because they are isolated from the decision making process. This isolation from the decision making process has led congregations to institutionalize the church thereby deviating from the model described and practiced in the first century. I am only writing about the decisions that affect the congregation as a whole. There are certainly situations when elders and deacons need to make decisions concerning the spiritual or personal welfare of the congregants in which the entire congregation does not need to be involved.

The three examples of decision making that are recorded in the Scriptures start as the apostles were waiting in the upper room for the promise of God (Acts 1). There was a need to replace Judas who had betrayed Jesus. A large group of disciples were present, among them the remaining eleven apostles. Peter called this need to replace Judas to their attention. They were of one mind on the matter, and they prayed about the situation that needed to be resolved.

To make this decision, first of all the need was identified, the qualifications of the replacement for Judas were put forth, and two men's names were put forth, Joseph called Barsabas and Matthias. God's providence was invoked through prayer, lots were cast, and Matthias was selected. The involvement of all the disciples created an atmosphere of peace and harmony. The Apostles did not presume to select the successor to Judas, but rather involved all of the disciples that were present, the soon to come "church."

The second example of decision making found in the New Testament was the selection of men to serve the needs of the Hellenistic widows (Acts 6:1-7). This problem was caused by the rapid growth of the early church. (Wouldn't it be great to have a problem today because of rapid growth in the church?) Again, the need was identified, the apostles and the disciples were involved, priorities were set, and seven men were selected to carry out the ministry of caring for these widows. The method of solving this problem was to summon the church and involve it in the decision making. Leadership identified the problem and gave the requirements to solve it. The congregation made the selection, and it was affirmed and prayed about by the apostles.

This exemplifies good leadership. This action pleased the whole multitude. The people were encouraged and the church grew. There was a keeping of the "unity of the Spirit" (Ephesians 4:3). This is an apostolic example of congregational involvement in making decisions that impact the congregation.

McGarvey (1892) wrote in his New Commentary on Acts of Apostles:

> It seemed good to the apostles and the Holy Spirit that the whole multitude of the disciples should take part in the selection of these officers, the apostles doing no more in the matter than to prescribe their qualifications. No ingenuity of argument can evade the conclusion that this gives the authority of apostolic precedent for the popular election of church officers. In what way the choice was made by the multitude, whether by balloting, or by a viva voice vote, and whether with or without nominations, we are not informed; and consequently, in reference to these points, every congregation is left to its own judgment. (pp. 104-105)

In Acts 15, we read of the third example of congregational involvement in decision making. The problem is identified as binding a portion of the Mosaic Law on new Gentile converts to Christianity that they be circumcised. The problem was taken to its source without any power struggle. There is open communication between leadership and the congregations. Paul and Barnabas and those that accompanied them "… were received by the church and the apostles and the elders…" (v. 4). The church was not excluded from hearing and seeking a solution to this problem.

Peter retold God's revelation to him concerning Cornelius (vv. 7-11), and Paul and Barnabas told of the miraculous signs and wonders that God performed among the Gentiles (v. 12). James reminded them of the Old Testament passages concerning the matter (vv. 13-18), and "Then the apostles and elders, with the whole congregation" (v. 22) reached a conclusion in response to God's revelation on the matter and communicated it back to the congregations at Antioch, Syria, and Cilicia.

David Lipscomb wrote:

> It is the right of every member of a congregation to know and to be heard in every work taken by that congregation.

> The elders are not to rule by arbitrary authority, as lords over God's heritage, but in all matters it is their duty to let every act of the congregation be known to all and to satisfy every one of the rightness of the proposed action, and to hear every man's objection and seek to remove them so as to lead them as examples of the flock, so that all may be united in one mind and one judgment and may as one body all work harmoniously and heartily to the same end. (David Lipscomb, Gospel Advocate, 1890, p. 119)

For congregational leaders, there are some questions that can be asked before making a decision that might ensure better understanding on the part of all concerned:

- Will God be glorified?
- Is it in the best spiritual interest of the church?
- Will it have positive spiritual ramifications for the church and for God?
- How is it linked to the Great Commission?
- Will it cost us more than money, for example, a good reputation, a good name, our souls?
- Are we serving the congregation in this matter or are we serving ourselves?
- How does the congregation feel about the matter?
- Has the congregation been informed and have we listened to its responses?

Leadership sets the tone of culture in an organization and leadership is also the catalyst for changing that culture. Do you see how these early church leaders influenced the culture of the early church in these three examples of decision making that we're given in the Scriptures? A closed meeting where the decisions concern the whole congregation seems out of place, especially in light of Apostolic example (Acts 1:15-26; 6:1-6; 15). Two-way conversations between decision makers and members of the group almost always have positive results.

For expediency sake, decisions may be made in a business meeting, where the congregation is represented by God-fearing, servants of Christ, and shepherds who know the sheep and are listening to the voice of the sheep. However, when this is the practice, it behooves the elders to communicate those decisions to the whole congregation in some fashion. An informed community has a higher probability of unification.

Another cultural norm of the first century was the refusal to bestow titles on church leaders. Moffatt (1938) in a study of the first five centuries of the church concluded that in the first three centuries Christians, "... continued to refuse the title of 'Lord' to anyone except Jesus Christ, who alone was to establish the divine Order [church] upon earth. It was their way of upholding what he stood for, at all costs, and they would not yield to any compromise in this issue any more than to subtler attempts in the direction of fusing their faith with non-political synergistic movements of the age" (p. 42). Jesus spoke of this in Matthew 23:9: "Do not call anyone on earth your father; for One is your Father, He who is in heaven." Jesus is referring to titles because of position and is not referring to biological fathers.

Many of the things we would like to know about the early first century Christian, we cannot know because these things are hidden by the curtain of time. By faith and by study, we can know what is in the Scriptures and this is enough to give us what we need to know about Christ, his work, and his plans for the church, its leadership, and our salvation.

The early Christians did not have a New Testament. They were taught by the apostles of Christ and his disciples as they were being baptized and added to the church. With this thought in mind, it is evident from the Scriptures that we do have, that teaching was of utmost importance and an integral part of the culture of the first century church. That teaching was also about Jesus and the salvation that he brought to the world, the gospel or good news.

I would encourage you to continue to look to the Scriptures for a continued study of these early Christians brothers and sisters and their culture and discern what is applicable to the church today. Is your congregation focused on learning from the early church or on innovations and change to that model thought to be necessary in today's church of the Lord?

Chapter 8
Shepherds, Elders, Bishops, or Overseers?

"Obey those who rule over you, and be submissive, for they watch out for your souls, as those who must give account. Let them do so with joy and not with grief, for that would be unprofitable for you" (Hebrews 13:17).

In today's world we are about two thousand years removed from the time that Christ lived among men and something less than two thousand years since the New Testament was written. When we examine any aspect of the Scriptures we have to keep that time difference in mind because the leadership role of elders must be understood in the context of those inspired writers' paradigms and the inspiration of God's Word. Our worldview is drastically different from those of that era. This is in part because the church has been institutionalized. This certainly does not mean that we need to bring the church up to date—it means that we need to remember Christ established only one church and that it is eternal and that man should not be about the business of changing the church but should be about the business of complying with God's Word on the organism, the church as it is described in the Scriptures.

Christ also reveals through his early followers and writers of the New Testament, a pattern of leaders for the local congregations. These men were referred to as elders, bishops, and pastors or shepherds depending on the function the inspired writers were writing about. The other term used for leaders in the first century church was deacons and described as those who ministered over the various work or ministries of the local congregation

(*The Open Bible*, 1997, p. 1738). These congregational leaders were to practice a servant leadership style.

Christ said, "Whoever would be great among you, let him be your servant" (Matthew 20:26). If anyone shows or proves himself in service (such as an elder or shepherd) then he is worthy to be obeyed and that service or servant leadership is his authority. It is bestowed by service and accepted by the congregants because of service. It is the functional role of the elder, bishop, pastor or shepherd, and deacons to serve in the context of the church of Christ as an organism. The style of a servant leader should be predominant in all Christians, especially those that are in the role of elders or deacons in congregations of the Lord's church.

Ferguson (1999) in his broad review of antiquity documents written in the first three centuries of Christendom found, in regard to elders, "The later books of the New Testament and the earliest post-apostolic writings indicate that at the end of the first century the general pattern of church organization was for local churches to be presided over by a plurality of elders, also called bishops, who were assisted by deacons" (p. 13). The references to elders in local congregations of Christ's church in the New Testament are also plural (Acts 14:23; Acts 15:2, 4, 6; I Timothy 5:17; and so forth). Therefore, in this writing, I will primarily use the term "elders" to refer to those men selected by the local congregation to be their leaders and provide spiritual oversight to the congregation; however, the terms shepherds, bishops, or pastors would all be just as appropriate from a scriptural perspective.

The term pastor is widely used today even though it only appears once in most translations, Ephesians 4:11, "And He Himself gave some *to be* apostles, some prophets, some evangelists, and some pastors and teachers." We should note here that this term is translated from *poimen*, meaning shepherds. First, the word is plural, pastors. It describes a function in the church and is not an office or title. Second, the first century pastor/shepherd does not relate in any fashion to the professionalized office we see today in many Christian religious groups. This usage is indicative of the institutionalization of the church and not to be found in the early church of Christ.

The "qualifications" of elders are found in Paul's letters to Timothy and Titus; these books are often referred to as the Pastoral Epistles by many religious scholars today. But, if we limit our study to just those epistles we are doing God's Word a grave injustice because there are lessons to be gleaned from many other passages in God's Word. I also suggest to the reader that we need to consider the "qualities" of elders, pastors, shepherds, and bishops and not just focus on "qualifications." When we focus on the qualities of these selected individuals to serve the congregation we mean those of peculiar or essential character.

I conducted a survey of about 100 folks who stated they were Christians. They identified three problems facing today's Christian groups. The first was that we are losing our children to worldly things. The second was that we do not retain those new Christians that become members. And the third problem identified was leadership. I would suggest to the reader that the first two problems are also related to leadership issues, either in the congregation or in the family structure. We have institutionalized the church and expect those men selected to be the various leaders to do all the things that a congregation should be doing as a body. Church leadership needs to take this issue and resolve it by teaching and training those of their respective flock what the Bible tells one about the duties of a Christian, a member of the body. The Scriptures should be examined constantly by the congregational leaders and members so that the church can be restored to the first century or New Testament model. Followership is just as important as leadership if not more so, because without followers we have no leaders. And training or teaching those that follow is just as important as training or developing leaders.

If we are to address the problem of "church" leadership, we must understand the structure of the church of Christ. To really understand the role of congregational leaders, we need to understand the role of shepherds, elders, bishops, or overseers, and we need to understand what the people of the first century understood about the role of a shepherd. A very good discourse on shepherding is found in the book of Ezekiel. Shepherding has not changed in undeveloped countries since that time and I suggest that maybe that's why God chose the metaphor of a shepherd to teach leaders of his people how they were to conduct themselves, because it was such an integral function of the time and is little changed over the centuries.

In Ezekiel 34 we find examples of wrong shepherding where the shepherds "feed themselves" instead of the sheep (v. 2) and "clothe themselves" while neglecting the flock (v. 3). They did not strengthen the weak (v. 4), neither did they heal those who were sick (v. 4), bind up the broken (v. 4), bring back those driven away (v. 4), or seek the lost (v. 4). We find that they did rule with force and cruelty (v. 4 and 21) and they did trample down the good pasture and "foul the clear waters" (v. 18). In other words they were selfish and self-serving.

The results of wrong shepherding can be devastating. Ezekiel wrote about what happens to a flock when it had bad shepherds or leadership: "they were scattered because there was no shepherd" (v. 5); "they become food for all the beasts" (v. 5); "they wandered…." (v. 6); and "no one was seeking or searching for them" (v. 6), so they "became a prey" (v. 8).

Ezekiel reveals to us that God's pronouncement against these false shepherds was: "Thus says the Lord God, Behold, I am against the shepherds…" (v. 9); "I will require My flock at their hand" (v. 9); "I will deliver My flock from their mouths…" (v. 9), and "I shall judge between sheep and sheep, between rams and goats" (v. 17).

We also find an excellent description of the good shepherd's work in Ezekiel 34. They are to search for the lost (v. 11), deliver them from being scattered (v. 12), and bring them to their own land (v. 13). Shepherds are to feed the flock in good pasture and provide a safe place for them so they can lie down in a good fold (v. 14). In addition they are to bring back those who have been driven away, bind the wounds of the wounded, and strengthen the sick (v. 16).

God will save the flock from evil shepherds (v. 22) by establishing Jesus as the good Shepherd (v. 23; John 10:11) and there will be a covenant of peace (v. 25). You see, God wants no bickering and division in the flock, the church. He wants peace because peace is unity and in unity the flock will grow and prosper.

Good shepherding brings about "showers of blessings" (v. 26) for the flock, the church. Good shepherding also results in fruitfulness, safety, knowledge of the Lord, and freedom (v. 27). Under good shepherds, the flock is no longer prey and they are not afraid (v. 28). Verse 29 indicates spiritual food or a spiritual feast will be provided by the shepherds and that there will be no shame. The flock will know that God is with them and know that they are God's people (v. 30). They will also know they belong to God and that he is their God (v. 31).

The tenth chapter of John also contains relevant material of shepherding, especially the "Good Shepherd." Jesus is being questioned by the Pharisees (chapter 9) and his response to them explained who he was and his relationship to our Father God. He also tells the Pharisees that there will be one flock and one shepherd describing the church and its head, Jesus Christ.

Now that we have a good idea of what shepherds meant to the people in the time of the first century, we can look to what the New Testament reveals about the shepherds, elders, bishops, or overseers of the church.

Remember the earlier discussion of the church as an organism where all members are equal (Rom. 12:4; I Corinthians 12)—they just have different functions predicated on their spiritual gifts (Rom. 12:6ff). By stating that all Christians are equal, I am not usurping the authority of elders or shepherds, I am merely stating that they have a different function based on their qualities and qualifications from other disciples in the congregation.

Serving as an elder is a particular function and is driven by one's desire to serve the congregation (I Timothy 3:1). In reference to the qualifications of elders in I Timothy 3, Lenski (1937) observed, "All the qualifications listed except aptness to teach and that pertaining to a novice are requirements that apply to all Christians" (p. 576). An elder, bishop, pastor, shepherd, overseer should exhibit strong servant leadership characteristics. But shouldn't all Christians exhibit strong leadership characteristics? Aren't we all commanded to serve Christ in evangelism, fellowship, and benevolence? If we do those things, we are examples to others, and as such we are leaders.

Jesus taught about servant leadership and about the work of shepherds. Christ said, "Whoever would be great among you, let him be your servant" (Matthew 20:26ff). If anyone shows or proves himself in service (such as an elder or shepherd) then he is worthy to be obeyed and that service or servant leadership is his authority. It is bestowed by service and accepted by the congregants because of service. It is the functional role of the elder, bishop, pastor, shepherd, overseer to serve the spiritual needs of the congregation in the context of the church of Christ as an organism.

In Ephesians 4, the apostle Paul stresses unity in the church, the church as an organism, and the leadership function of equipping members for ministry. It was the role of apostles (unfortunately there are no longer any with us), prophets (and again there are no longer any with us), evangelists, pastors or shepherds, and teachers, to equip the saints or Christians for the work of ministry and edification of the body, the organism, the church. Because we no longer have apostles and prophets, it falls upon evangelists or preachers; pastors or shepherds, elders, bishops, or overseers; and teachers to perform the ministry of equipping the saints or members of the church for the various ministries that need to be carried out in order for the church to grow. This is an important aspect of the church because when "every part does its share, [it] causes growth of the body for the edifying of itself in love" (Ephesians 4:16). I believe if this were the case in congregations of believers, the responses to my survey would have been much different.

Elder, bishop, overseer, pastor, and shepherd are terms used interchangeably in the New Testament and their role or function is primarily to be responsible for the souls of the congregation—an awesome responsibility. There are definitions or explanations of words that we need to understand so that we can understand that they all refer to the same people—the ones who serve the congregation in the ministry of spiritual guidance, the elder, bishop, pastor, shepherd, overseer.

The Greek word *presbuteros*, the Latin word *presbyter*, and the Anglo-Saxon word *elder* all literally mean 'one who is older.' There was, however, a secondary meaning based on the custom of having the older men of a village function as the decision-makers for the village (Yeakley, 1980, p. 18). Therefore, "This secondary meaning of the word 'elder' referred to a decision-making, policy-making, executive function" (Yeakley, 1980, p. 18). But remember that an effective eldership would involve the congregation in those decisions that involve the congregation as a whole.

"The Greek word *episkopos*, the Latin word *bishop*, and the Anglo-Saxon word *overseer* all refer to an administrative function" (Yeakley, 1980, p. 18).

"The Greek word *poimen*, the Latin word *pastor*, and the Anglo-Saxon word *shepherd* all literally mean 'one who tends a flock of sheep'" (Yeakley, 1980, p. 20). Ephesians 4:11 is the only occurrence of the use of poimen/ pastor in the New Testament but yet it has become widely spread to denote the one leader of many protestant groups. In its one usage in the New Testament, it is also plural suggesting that there would be more than one pastor or shepherd in the congregation.

The leadership of any organization is charged with providing the vision or direction for the organization and this guidance is certainly needed in congregations of the Lord. That vision is contained within the Scriptures of the New Testament and congregations of the Lord should have that vision before them at all times. Providing vision to the local congregation is a function of the elders with the input of the congregants or members of any local congregation that follows the pattern of the New Testament church. "Where there is no vision, the people perish" (Proverbs 29:18).

There is a need for the various congregations of the church to have elders and those elders to accept that function which includes the function of the spiritual oversight of the congregation. However, in those Christian groups that do have elders they often select elders based on their business wisdom and leadership in the secular world. Then if they have some knowledge of the Scriptures and exhibit some of the qualities of a spiritual leader, they are thought to be a good choice to serve as elder or shepherd. James warns us about this when he asked the question, "Who is wise and understanding among you?" (James 3:13). James goes on to warn Christians about wisdom from a worldly perspective and tell us we should look for wisdom that is from above because it "is first pure, then peaceable, gentle, willing to yield, full of mercy and good fruits, without partiality and without hypocrisy" (James 3:17). Now, I don't want to imply that James is simply addressing wisdom in elders because he is not—he is addressing wisdom in all Christians. Therefore, this wisdom from above should surely apply to our elders if we want them to lead us spiritually with wisdom from above! Many times when we select elders to oversee the work of the congregation, we institutionalize the church just as we do when we select special ministers or deacons to serve the needs of the congregation because we then say the elders should do this and the deacons should do that when the reality of the New Testament is that all Christians are to do the work of the church. The elders are to function as spiritual leaders and the deacons are to lead the congregation in the work of the congregation in its various ministries. Neither of them is to do ALL the work of the congregation themselves, they are to lead that work and be part of it along with other Christians. All members of a congregation are to be involved in the work of the congregation, but not necessarily be involved in all the work of the congregation simply because their gifts and/or functions in the organism must be considered and we all have a different number and variety of gifts/talents.

In New Testament times it was God's plan that every church should have a plurality of elders to direct and oversee its members. This is still the case today because there was only one church established. There were elders in the church at Jerusalem, as we learn from Acts 15:2, and in the churches of Judaea, as shown by the following passage: "Then the disciples, every man according to his ability, determined to send relief unto the brethren that dwelt in Judaea: Which also they did, and sent it to the elders by the hands of Barnabas and Saul" (Acts 11:29, 30). There were also a plurality of elders in the church at Ephesus (Acts 20:17). A search of the word elder and elders found three occurrences of the word *elder* and 60 occurrences of the word *elders* in the New Testament in the New King James translation.

Some of the examples of a plurality of elders are when Paul and Barnabas were returning from their missionary journey, in addition to their preaching and confirming the souls of the brethren, the record says: "And when they had ordained them elders in every church, and had prayed with fasting, they commended them to the Lord, on whom they believed' (Acts 14:23). In Paul's letter to Titus we read: "For this reason I left you in Crete, that you should set in order the things that are lacking, and appoint elders in every city as I commanded you" (Titus 1:5).

From the above Scriptures we understand that it is God's desire that there be a plurality of elders in every congregation of the church of the Lord. Hence we should try to meet God's requirements in doing his work. I would not say that a church could not exist without elders, but there is something wrong with any church which cannot in a reasonable time develop men for this great work (Grimsley, 1964).

The function or ministry for governing the church that Jesus left on earth has been vested in the role or function of the eldership of the church. When elders or shepherds are selected by a congregation, those congregants fall under the oversight of those whom they have selected. Paul said: "But we beseech you, brethren, to know them that labor among you, and are over you in the Lord, and admonish you; and to esteem them exceedingly highly in love for their work's sake" (I Thessalonians 5:12, 13). Again: "Let the elders that rule well be counted worthy of double honor, especially those who labor in the word and in teaching" (I Timothy 5:17). And again: "Remember them that had the rule over you, men that spake unto you the Word of God; and considering the issue of their life, imitate their faith" (Hebrews 13:7). "Obey them that have the rule over you, and submit to them: for they watch in behalf of your souls, as they that shall give account; that they may do this with joy, and not with grief: for this were unprofitable for you" (Hebrews 13:17). We also need to remember that all members of the organism are equal, but there are different functions and serving as an elder or shepherd of a congregation is the function of the ones selected so we need to then become their followers as long as they adhere to the duties as described in the Scriptures. For emphasis I again say, without good followers we would not have good leaders; there is an interrelationship between leaders and followers.

There is no instruction in the New Testament on how elders are to be appointed or selected. Acts 6:1-6 gives us a clue that men were called out by the congregation to do the work of the church; however, there is no inference that those called out in that particular instance were deacons or elders although it is a widely accepted view that this is an example of the choosing of deacons. The apostles told the congregation to choose these men to serve. They are never referred to as deacons in the Scriptures but the basic assumption is that they were in fact deacons. We are instructed to have elders, we have the qualifications (we also need to consider their qualities) for elders, and it is up to the local congregation as to how those qualified men are to be selected or appointed.

The qualities for elders are given to us in I Timothy 3:1-7 and again in Titus 1:5-9. I would urge all members of the church of Christ to read and study these as well as other Scriptures dealing with this congregational function, not just when you're in the process of identifying men to serve the congregation in this capacity or function, but on a regular basis. This leadership development should extend to all members of the congregation who desire to be ministers of any congregational work. It is impossible to have good, effective servant leaders without good, effective followership.

The qualities that an elder should exhibit are to desire the ministry of serving the congregation as an elder, be blameless, be the husband of one wife, temperate, sober-minded, be of good behavior, hospitable, and able to teach. He should not be given to wine, not violent, and not greedy for money. He should be gentle in nature, not one to quarrel with others, and not covetous. He should govern his own house well and have believing children. He should not be a novice or new Christian because serving in this capacity might make him prideful. He should last of all have a good reputation in the community in which he resides and works so that he doesn't reflect badly on the church of our Lord. Another look at Ezekiel 34 provides some additional advice or qualities for good shepherds as well as some warning about bad shepherds. We would do well to heed these sayings.

Paul also implies as he writes to Timothy that an elder should be worthy of his wages (I Timothy 5:17). This is the only indication that I have found of any wages for anyone involved in the activities of the church during the first century but in today's Christian groups we find most of the congregational budget going to pay the salaries of the preachers, evangelists, and other congregational staff as well as those salaries of those in the hierarchal structures of their governance staff, another indication of the institutionalization of the church. I haven't found any literature that determined when the practice of paying church leaders and staff started as a practice.

The elders or shepherds, with input from the congregation, should provide a clear, concise strategic statement or vision of the congregation's mission and with direction or focus on the work and activity of the congregation. Followers should be caught up in the vision, mission, and direction of the congregation as ones who have co-ownership. These vision and mission statements should be linked to the Great Commission (Matthew 28:18-20) as it is the mission of the church and was commanded by Jesus.

It is important that leaders demonstrate the style of leadership that Jesus taught his apostles and disciples—that of a servant. People do not react well to a directive or autocratic style of leadership. Directive or autocratic leadership also causes frustration in the congregation, resentment, apathy, and a "we-they" mindset that is contrary to the unity that is taught in God's Word. This style of leadership will cause the congregation to not reach its fullest potential in reaching out and teaching others the good news—the gospel of Christ. Jesus himself warned against this style of leadership in Matthew 20:25 and Mark 10:42. The leader who serves well will develop followers that serve well.

The major emphasis in the church of Christ should be one of service at all levels of the congregation—the emphasis should not be on control or position or authority. Remember, "the son of man came not to be served but to serve" (Matthew 20:28) and he was one who, in fact, served (Luke 22:27).

When we select elders, we tend to focus on college education or business acumen along with some knowledge of the Bible to determine if one "qualifies" as an elder. We need, instead, to look at their qualities, not qualifications, to determine if they are suitable to be asked to lead the congregation in matters of a spiritual or scriptural nature. Qualities are a measure of a man's character while qualifications have become a checklist. We need to take a longer period of time, as well, in the selection process of elders and deacons. We need to discuss and review the qualities that are found in the Scriptures about elders and deacons instead of concentrating on qualifications. It's not enough to know the qualifications of the individual under consideration, we need to know and understand the qualities that make up the character of each individual under consideration. Qualifications can be apparent on the surface and lost internally, while looking at character qualities of the individual tells us about that person's self. For example, do they visit the sick to check off the qualification or do they visit the sick out of concern for their fellow man and fellow Christian (James 5:14-15).

As followers of Christ and as members of a congregation that strives to serve him, we need to be mindful of Paul's words to Timothy. "Let the elders who rule well be counted worthy of double honor, especially those who labor in the word and doctrine. For the Scriptures say, *'You shall not muzzle an ox while it treads out the grain,'* and, 'The laborer *is* worthy of his wages.' Do not receive an accusation against an elder except from two or three witnesses. Those who are sinning rebuke in the presence of all, that the rest also may fear" (I Timothy 5:17-21). As we follow Christ we must follow the elders that are filling the functional role of spiritual leaders in a scripturally organized congregation.

Remember, there is only one church (Ephesians 4:4). Elders who serve the various congregations that are attempting to model the church of Christ as depicted in the New Testament should also remember that they are equal members of the organism, the church of Christ and as such, they serve the spiritual needs of the congregation and should not take up busy work such as planning buildings, cleaning buildings, picking colors to paint the walls, and deciding when the grass needs cutting so that they appear to function as an elder. Elders need to teach congregants that all the members of the congregation are to come together to worship, to edify one another, and to do the benevolent work of the congregation.

I interviewed a dozen ministers or preachers of various religious groups and those that labored in congregations that had elders said that the current problem with most elderships is that they act as a board of directors. The Baptist ministers and Presbyterian ministers (50% of sample) actually stated that was the function of the eldership while those who were ministers in the Lord's church (50% of sample) said there was movement in that direction in that religious group as well, another indication of the institutionalization of the church. The elders hire the minister or preacher; therefore, they expect him to take on some of the role of "overseeing" the flock, visiting the sick, and so forth because they, the elders, are busy with business and other responsibilities. These ministers and preachers also stated leadership was a major problem in most congregations of the church.

They also saw the problems facing church leaders today as: demands for change, the traditional views of the family are under attack, and women's roles in the church. Contemporary society has radically changed over the last several decades and demands change in the organizations in which they are active participants. People no longer can be expected to accept the traditional leadership methods without straight answers from their leaders. Religious leaders have to step up and teach the scriptural model of leadership and followership if the church, as described in the New Testament, is to survive. Today there is gender and generational segmentation in families. Church leaders take great risk if they ignore the generation gaps of the congregation and the social influence to be more accepting of those with "different lifestyles." They must be addressed in a scriptural context. Women's demands for more involvement in leadership roles have been influenced by the societal shift in women's roles in the secular world. Women were certainly involved with the first century church and Ferguson (1995) writes, "In orthodox, mainstream circles the same situation prevailed as that reflected in the New Testament documents: a very full involvement of women in every aspect of the church's life except speaking in the public liturgical assemblies and serving as elders/bishops" (p. 235).

This is by no means a definitive study of the function of elders but it will get one started exploring the role of elders if the Scriptures are the basis of the study and if one keeps the biases and experiences of the world at bay while examining what the Word of Christ reveals to the astute student. Elders serving congregations that worship in the spirit and pattern of the first century church are to be respected, followed, and recognized for their service to the congregation and to the Word of God.

Chapter 9
Deacons and Ministry Leaders

"Now in those days, when the number of the disciples was multiplying, there arose a complaint against the Hebrews by the Hellenists, because their widows were neglected in the daily distribution. Then the twelve summoned the multitude of the disciples and said, "It is not desirable that we should leave the word of God and serve tables. Therefore, brethren, seek out from among you seven men of good reputation, full of the Holy Spirit and wisdom, whom we may appoint over this business; but we will give ourselves continually to prayer and to the ministry of the word."

"And the saying pleased the whole multitude. And they chose Stephen, a man full of faith and the Holy Spirit, and Philip, Prochorus, Nicanor, Timon, Parmenas, and Nicolas, a proselyte from Antioch, whom they set before the apostles; and when they had prayed, they laid hands on them" (Acts 6:1-6).

First, in looking at the function of deacons, we must realize that a deacon serves the congregation is some way and should also be viewed as a minister. A minster equates to one who is a servant. As a matter of fact, all Christians should be viewed as ministers and as servants. In writing of the qualifications of elders and deacons, as recorded in I Timothy 3, Lenski (1937) stated, "All the qualifications listed except aptness to teach and that pertaining to a novice are requirements that apply to all Christians" (p. 576).

This is the approach that I have taken as a result of my study of the New Testament church of Christ. The deacon does not fill an office or position in the church, but fills a function that is needed in the organism to carry out the work of the church. Another thing that is important about deacons as well as elders or bishops is that they are different from the other members of the congregation as noted by Paul (Philippians 1:1). They are different because they have a different function in the body, not because they hold position or office in the congregation.

Most Bible scholars accept the notion that the first deacons were selected to fulfill a specific need in the early church as depicted in the Acts 6:1-7 even though this notion is not revealed in the Scriptures. The apostles told the congregation in Jerusalem to pick out seven good men to do this work of the church so that they, the Apostles, would be free to perform their function. The apostles continued to teach and preach and spread the Word of God (Acts 6:7) while those selected men took care of the needs of the Hellenist widows. We do our elders an injustice today by looking to them to make decisions and be involved in issues that they should not be involved with, issues that deacons or other members could take upon themselves to handle. We do this because we have institutionalized the church as a result of perceiving the church as having a similar organizational structure as the organizations we see in the world. That is not the structure of the church according to God's Scriptures. God's structure for the church is that of an organism where all the members are equal but have different functions based on the gifts they have been given.

Based on Acts 6, the function of a deacon seems to be one of leading ministries in which the local congregation is involved. In many cases, there is little attention on the work of deacons. They are selected to serve the congregation, given a ministry to oversee, and then micromanaged by the elders or other church leaders. The shame of it is that most of them want to serve the congregation and the work of the church. I will never forget the words of a young man that a congregation had asked to serve as a deacon. When asked by the elders about his capacity to serve, he responded, "If the congregation desires me to serve them, and I am scripturally qualified, then I would be remiss if I did not serve God in this capacity. I believe it would be a sin for me not to serve."

We need legions of men and women in the church with this attitude. All Christians should have this attitude. We would see much growth in the Lord's body if this were the case.

The word, *deacon*, appears five times in the New King James translation of the Bible; however, the Greek word, *diakonos,* from which deacon is translated appears 32 times. Twenty times it is rendered *minister*, seven times it is translated *servant*, and five times it is translated *deacon.* In all cases it is referring to service, and again I remind the reader that all Christians should be functioning as ministers and servants.

In I Timothy 3:8-13, Paul lists the qualifications of deacons and when we couple those qualities with Acts 6:1-7, a picture emerges of one who will be a servant and minister to the needs and works of the congregation. Their work is defined by the Greek word *diakonos*: to serve, to minister, and to be helpers. In Matthew 20:28 Jesus said he came to be a servant or deacon, *diskonos*. What better model is there for a deacon or minister than that of Jesus. For that matter, Jesus is the absolute model for all Christians.

Congregations can use Acts 6:1-7 as the model for selecting deacons. First of all the church was summoned (v. 2) and the church leaders (in this case, apostles) told the church to "seek out from among you seven" men to serve in the function of serving the widows that were being neglected. The congregation of the church was advised of the qualities that these individuals should have: "of *good* reputation, full of the Holy Spirit and wisdom" (v. 3). When these men were appointed it "pleased the whole multitude" (v. 5). Some points to be learned are: the process involved the whole congregation; the congregation worked under the direction of the apostles (today it should be under the direction of elders/bishops/shepherds/pastors); there were prayers during the process; and the involvement of everyone promoted congregational unity, harmony, and cooperation. The church grew as a result. The personal qualities of a deacon must be considered, not just a qualification checklist when a congregation is going through the process of selecting men to lead its various ministries.

These qualities according to I Timothy 3:8-13 are "grave" meaning that the person should be dignified or of a serious mind. He should also not be "double-tongued" or one who talks out of both sides of his mouth—saying one thing to one person and another thing to another person. He should also exhibit honesty, integrity, and dependability.

He should be "not given to much wine." No priest could serve when drinking intoxicating drink (Leviticus 10:8-11). All Christians are priests and are continually serving (Romans 12:1-2) so the deacon and elder are not singled out in this respect; all Christians should abstain from intoxicating drink and other mind altering drugs. The deacon should not be covetous or a lover of money—"not greedy of filthy lucre." His heart should be focused on spiritual things, not materialism. He should be a faithful Christian, "holding the mystery of the faith in a pure conscience," and "not a novice" or recent convert. He should be "blameless" or not guilty of consciously committing sin.

His wife must also exhibit these Christian values or characteristics. The deacon should be the "husband of one wife" and "rule well his own house." As stated earlier, ideally all Christians would exhibit these characteristics or values.

The work of a deacon is suggested by the very word; diakonos, translated deacon, which means to serve, to minister, or to be helpers. In Acts 6 we know the men selected were to look after the Hellenistic widows. In Acts 7:1ff we find Stephen, one of the seven, preaching God's Word so he was doing the work of an evangelist also. In I Timothy 3:13 we read, "For those who have served well as deacons obtain for themselves a good standing and great boldness in the faith which is in Christ Jesus."

The work of a deacon (and all Christians) should exemplify Christ, for Matthew wrote the words of Jesus, "… the Son of Man did not come to be served, but to serve, and to give His life a ransom for many" (Matthew 20:28). That makes work of the church a glorious effort and we should all be doing so with capable deacons or other ministers leading that work while the elders care for the spiritual well-being of the congregation. Jesus said that serving was the route to real greatness (Matthew 20:26). Deacons as well as all members of the congregation of the Lord's body should work under the oversight of the elders and should be submissive to them (Hebrews 13:17).

Deacons should serve according to the gifts they receive from God through the Holy Spirit. All members of the Lord's body are equal but have different functions according to their respective talents or gifts (Romans 12). Every member of a congregation should use or exercise their respective gifts in order to grow and to increase their talents.

The next ministry leader or minister we will examine is the evangelist. This term is used in II Timothy 4:1-5, Acts 21:8, and Ephesians 4:5. It is translated from the Greek *euangelistes* and denotes an evangelist, a messenger of the gospel, one who proclaims the good news of Christ. Evangelists are not to be confused with administrators or pastors or elders because any Christian could be an evangelist if they have the gift for it.

Again, this term describes a function and not an "office." The task or function of the evangelist is to "preach the word" (II Timothy 4:2) or preach the gospel. It is not an administrative function.

> The apostle Paul was exhorting or encouraging young Timothy to: Preach the word! Be ready in season *and* out of season. Convince, rebuke, exhort, with all longsuffering and teaching. For the time will come when they will not endure sound doctrine, but according to their own desires, *because* they have itching ears, they will heap up for themselves teachers; and they will turn *their* ears away from the truth, and be turned aside to fables. But you be watchful in all things, endure afflictions, do the work of an evangelist, fulfill your ministry. (II Timothy 4:2-5)

Timothy was an evangelist but Paul also warned him that the time would come when the people would not endure sound doctrine; they would turn to false teachers. The Scriptures reveal this began to happen in the first century church almost immediately (see I Corinthians 1; Revelation 2:12-17). Jesus warned of these false teachers in Matthew 7:15, "Beware of false prophets, who come to you in sheep's clothing, but inwardly they are ravenous wolves." He said we would know them by their fruits. Paul, Peter, and John all warn of false teachers or prophets in their respective epistles.

The works of the evangelists were evident in the writings of Origen when in *Against Celus* 3.9 he wrote "Some Christians have made it their work to travel around not only to cities but also to villages and country houses in order to make others pious toward God. And one would not say that they did this on account of money, when they would not even accept their sustenance" (as cited in Ferguson, 1999, pp. 166-167). Ferguson also quotes Eusebius concerning evangelism: "Then setting out on their journey they performed the work of evangelists, being zealous to preach to those who had not yet heard the word of faith and to deliver to them the written form of the Divine Gospels" (p. 167). It appears that in the first century church, evangelists were involved in carrying the word to the world while elders were concerned with the internal teaching. An excellent goal for evangelists would be some of Paul's advice to Timothy, "Take heed to yourself and to the doctrine. Continue in them, for in doing this you will save both yourself and those who hear you" (I Timothy 4:16).

Another minister of function of some in the church is that of a preacher, also one who proclaims the gospel of Jesus Christ (Acts 8:5). Paul describes himself as a preacher in his first letter to Timothy, "For *there is* one God and one Mediator between God and men, *the* Man Christ Jesus, who gave Himself a ransom for all, to be testified in due time, for which I was appointed a preacher and an apostle—I am speaking the truth in Christ *and* not lying—a teacher of the Gentiles in faith and truth" (I Timothy 1:5-7). Paul also tells his protégé Timothy to preach (II Timothy 4:2). The qualifications of preachers and evangelists are the same and Christians today need to know and understand that in the first century church, these individuals were focused on unbelieving persons external to the church as their function, and not as chaplains to the congregation. We also see in the example of Paul that he filled two functions in the early church, that of an apostle and that of a preacher; another great lesson for the Christian who holds the view that since we have preachers to preach, deacons to serve the congregation, elders or shepherds to oversee the flock, all I have to do is attend the occasional worship service in the capacity of a spectator to be entertained.

Evangelizing and preaching should be about announcing the Good News of salvation and is translated from the Greek word, euangelizesthai. It is found 55 times in the New Testament and is translated "preach" 23 times; "preach the gospel" 22 times; "show glad tidings" two times, and "bring good tidings" two times.

Again, I posit that we have institutionalized the church today and that most congregations have evangelists or preachers that serve the function of a chaplain instead of proclaiming the gospel externally to unbelievers, those who are in a lost state. We have adopted a "pastoral" structure in the church in some cases where the authority of the elders has been relegated to the "pastor" or preacher or evangelist while the elders do the work of the deacons and the deacons are either micromanaged or non-functional as ministry leaders. We need to examine the Scriptures and restore the church by following the functions and guidelines contained therein.

McDaniel (1921) wrote that the church is "A body equal in rank and privilege. … Officers are chosen for service not for dictation, for leadership not for lordship" (p. 25). This holds true for all who would lead a ministry. Many of the folks I have interviewed regarding the church today speak of the petty jealousies displayed by various ministers and the many names they bestow on themselves in order to gain recognition. It should not be so in the church. Ministry leaders, as well as all Christians, should be servants.

Too little attention has been given to the work of a deacon and others that minister in the Lord's work. "We" appoint men as deacons or ministers over some work, then we do not give them a job to do or they are micromanaged. They often just wear a name and sit on the sidelines, wondering how to serve and what to do. The shame is that most of them want to serve, be involved in doing the work of a deacon. This well may be our weakest point in restoring New Testament Christianity.

When Jesus was training the apostles to take the leadership role in the church, he sent them out into the world with explicit instructions (Matthew 10). He sent forth the twelve and then later he sent forth seventy (Luke 10). If Jesus saw the need for the development of church leaders, shouldn't every congregation of the Lord have a leadership development plan in place? This sort of training needs to start early and be a perpetual program of study in order that congregations are equipped with appropriate leaders whenever the need arises.

I'll finish this chapter with one account of an experience I encountered concerning church leadership. I was asked to preach for a congregation that had lost its preacher. I did not have any prior knowledge of this congregation, but when I arrived that morning there were more than fifty folks present for Bible study. I was put on the spot and asked to teach that class without prior notice. As I taught the class, there were several men in the audience that commented extensively and scripturally about the lesson, demonstrating their great depth of knowledge of God's Word.

For the morning worship hour another twenty-five or so souls gathered and I delivered the sermon I had prepared. I had been prompted to be prepared to stay for the evening worship hour as well and was pleasantly surprised when more than half those in attendance for the morning service also attended the evening service. After both the morning and evening service, I was engaged in further discussion of the topics I had delivered to the extent that I began to wonder why one of the local men had not been utilized to preach and teach in these services. The gentleman who had approached me about preaching and teaching was present so I simply asked him why none of the apparently qualified men were not utilized to teach and preach instead of asking me to be there.

He confirmed that there were several men in the congregation that could have filled the need but that they refused to do so. I was reminded of Paul's instructions to young Timothy: "Preach the word! Be ready in season *and* out of season. Convince, rebuke, exhort, with all longsuffering and teaching" (II Timothy 4:2). I view this instruction to Timothy to be applicable to all men who have matured as Christians. These men in my story were spectators and not really involved. What a shame! This account demonstrates anecdotally why I posit that leadership development programs are needed in every congregation of the Lord.

Chapter 10
Women of the New Testament

"And many of the Samaritans of that city believed in Him because of the word of the woman who testified, 'He told me all that I ever did'"
(John 4:39).

Today we see much controversy concerning the role of women in the various Christian religious groups. To understand the woman's role, as with any other role, it's important to closely examine the most relevant evidence of women's roles in the church described in the New Testament and then the reader needs to compare those findings to whatever group he or she is affiliated with today. When an organization, in this study—the organism or church of Christ—is examined through the eyes of organization development, the study of the founding leader and current leadership of that organization is essential to understand the culture and subsequently the meaning of the organization. In this case it is the same being. We know that Jesus founded the church and we know that Jesus is still head of his church so we will look to his teachings and examples that involved women during his life here on earth in the form of a man. We will not look at other writings of men except when related to the first century church.

We must also examine the whole of any document (in our study, the New Testament) which guides the church in its beliefs and values. Everything must be examined in context. The New Testament is the new and better covenant from Jesus and it takes away the Old Testament laws and rules (Hebrews 8.1-13). Christians live under the New Testament or the new covenant and under that covenant we're told:

> For you are all sons of God through faith in Christ Jesus. For as many of you as were baptized into Christ have put on Christ. There is neither Jew nor Greek, there is neither slave nor free, there is neither male nor female; for you are all one in Christ Jesus. And if you *are* Christ's, then you are Abraham's seed, and heirs according to the promise. (Galatians 3:26-29)

Remember that these are God's words given to us through the pen of the Apostle Paul. Paul is revealing a fact to the Galatian church that all Christians are equal in the church. He also tells the Corinthian Christians this same message in I Corinthians chapter 11 when he presents the metaphor of an organism or body to demonstrate the structure of the church.

Jesus Christ is the head of the organism that is the church that was initiated after his crucifixion and resurrection (Eph. 4:15). What he did when he lived among mankind is important to understand as well as the underlying beliefs and values that shaped the birth of his church and its congregants in the first century. In observing the woman's role in the church of Christ, Jesus' trip through Samaria early in his earthly ministry (John 4:1-45), reveals that he used a woman in a positive way to deliver his message to her village. Jesus and his disciples were traveling from Judea to Galilee and the Scriptures tell us he needed to go through Samaria (v. 4) but it doesn't reveal to us why he needed to go through Samaria. Perhaps it was another teaching opportunity where his disciples would see that Jesus did not hold the Samaritans in the same negative light the Jewish people did (v. 9), or perhaps it was to teach them something about Jesus' viewpoint of women. I don't know why but I do know that had it been important for us to know why Jesus chose to go through Samaria it would have been reveled through the inspired writers.

Jesus and his disciples were about the business of making disciples and baptizing them (v. 1). Jesus offered the living water to the Samaritan woman he met at the well (v. 10-14) and then used her to tell the men of Sychar about him, Jesus, and that he was at the well (v. 28-30). He used her even though she had had five husbands and was apparently living with another man at that time (v. 17-18). Many of the Samaritans, when they heard Jesus' teachings, believed in Jesus (v. 39), encouraged him to stay with them (v. 40), and as a result of his staying and teaching many more came to believe in him (v. 41). As a practitioner of organization development observing this scenario, I have to conclude that Jesus expected women to be active in spreading the gospel and that he used this scenario to teach this principle to his disciples that were traveling with him.

The inspired writers, Matthew and Mark, also write that Jesus cast a demon from a Gentile woman's daughter because of the woman's great faith even though she was a Gentile (Matthew 15:21-28; Mark 7:24-30). This is an indication to his disciples that Gentiles (even though they didn't recognize it at the time) would ultimately have the gospel delivered to them. It is important that Jesus reveals his attitude about women and Gentiles when he uses her faith as the basis for his healing the woman's daughter.

We also know from Luke's writings that women who had been converted to Jesus' teachings traveled with him and his twelve disciples. This passage follows:

> Now it came to pass, afterward, that He went through every city and village, preaching and bringing the glad tidings of the kingdom of God. And the twelve *were* with Him, and certain women who had been healed of evil spirits and infirmities—Mary called Magdalene, out of whom had come seven demons, and Joanna the wife of Chuza, Herod's steward, and Susanna, and many others who provided for Him from their substance. (Luke 8:1-3)

We are not told why these women were traveling with Jesus and the twelve but I'm sure that some would say their function was to cook and take care of these traveling disciples; however, there is no evidence of that in the Scriptures either—we just know that the women provided "from their substance." Were these women publicly supporting and funding mission work? As we look at these women's dedication and commitment to Jesus, we also find later that some of them were there in his last hours, watched his crucifixion, and were the first to see him resurrected.

We also find that Jesus often used women as principal characters in the parables that he used to teach. For example:

> Then He spoke a parable to them, that men always ought to pray and not lose heart, saying: "There was in a certain city a judge who did not fear God nor regard man. Now there was a widow in that city; and she came to him, saying,

> 'Get justice for me from my adversary.' And he would not for a while; but afterward he said within himself, 'Though I do not fear God nor regard man, yet because this widow troubles me I will avenge her, lest by her continual coming she weary me.'"

Then the Lord said, "Hear what the unjust judge said. And shall God not avenge His own elect who cry out day and night to Him, though He bears long with them? I tell you that He will avenge them speedily. Nevertheless, when the Son of Man comes, will He really find faith on the earth?." (Luke 18:1-8) (Also see Matthew 25:1-13 and Luke 15:8-10.)

A woman was also the principal character to demonstrate generosity when she anointed Jesus' feet with "very costly oil of spikenard" while Judas' true character of greediness was put on display (John 12:1-7). There are other instances of women playing important roles during the days when Jesus was on the earth in the body of a man and we need to examine all these Scriptures in studying the role of women in the church, but you, the reader, will have to do that on your own because of limited space in this book.

Now let's look at the woman's role during the time that Jesus was first laid in the tomb by Joseph. They observed his body in the tomb (Luke 23:55) and they went and obtained things to prepare his body and returned to the tomb to do so (Luke 23:56). They then returned to the tomb on the first day of the week to further prepare the body by adding spices but they found the rock rolled away and the tomb empty of the body of Jesus (Luke 24:1-3). These very women then went and informed the eleven remaining disciples/apostles that Jesus was missing from the tomb (Luke 24:9). These women were named Mary Magdalene, Joanna, Mary the mother of James [and Jesus], and other women (Luke 24:10). Why did Jesus or his Father not assign this very important discovery to some of the men, even to the apostles? I don't know the answer to that question but what I do know is that women were a very integral part of the discovery that Jesus had risen from the dead.

Now we need to turn to the Scriptures that came into being during the first century of the church's existence and have been preserved for us in the bible. The verses that cause much controversy concerning women's role in the various Christian religious groups are I Corinthians 14:34-35 and I Timothy 2:11-14 and these are the verses of Scripture that some see as "limiting" the roles of women in the church. I do not see the role of women as being limited; I just see that they have a different function within the organism. We will talk about these two passages of Scripture later but first let's examine some other passages about the things that women were doing in the first century church.

First of all Paul tells us, "Now the Lord is the Spirit; and where the Spirit of the Lord *is,* there *is* liberty" (II Cor. 3:17). I pose this question in reference to this statement: Is the position that the Lord is Spirit and wherever the Spirit of the Lord is, there is liberty or freedom compatible with I Corinthians 14:34-35? When we examine the already mentioned passage Galatians 3:26-29 and Paul's very explicit description of the church as an organism in I Corinthians 12:12-31 where all members of the body are equal and all the members of the body have respective gifts as described in I Corinthians 12:1-11 with I Corinthians 14:34-35 and I Timothy 2:11-14, there seems to me to be much dichotomy between these verses and so we need to examine why is there this dichotomy.

Paul discusses public prayer in I Corinthians 11:1-34 with much detail and it appears that women prayed in that time in public (v.5). This discussion also centers on a woman's head being covered but Paul describes that covering in verse 15 when he wrote, "But if a woman has long hair, it is a glory to her; for *her* hair is given to her for a covering." I have heard many debates about women covering their head when they're in the worship service but this passage of Scripture clearly says that the covering for her head is her hair. One time when traveling my wife and I stopped in at a church that was not familiar to us and as soon as the worship service began, many of the women pulled out little scarves or handkerchiefs and covered their head. Paul clearly writes that there is no such custom in the church of God (v. 16). It appears to me that Paul is teaching that a woman's appearance should not be such that she would appear to be a man instead of a woman. Paul issues many warnings to the church in this particular passage but he does not mention women being silent in the church here. He goes on to describe the gifts of the Spirit and the organism, pointing out that all members are equal, and then tells us that we should abide in faith, hope, and love and that the greatest of these is love (I Corinthians 12 and 13).

Paul wrote to the church at Ephesus concerning their gifts and that they were to all be united in faith and that the body, the church of Christ, was knit and joined together in such a manner that the body was effective and grew when all members did their share.

> "And He Himself gave some *to be* apostles, some prophets, some evangelists, and some pastors and teachers, for the

> equipping of the saints for the work of ministry, for the edifying of the body of Christ, till we all come to the unity of the faith and of the knowledge of the Son of God, to a perfect man, to the measure of the stature of the fullness of Christ; that we should no longer be children, tossed to and fro and carried about with every wind of doctrine, by the trickery of men, in the cunning craftiness of deceitful plotting, but, speaking the truth in love, may grow up in all things into Him who is the head—Christ—from whom the whole body, joined and knit together by what every joint supplies, according to the effective working by which every part does its share, causes growth of the body for the edifying of itself in love." (Ephesians 4:11-16)

This passage includes women as members and so it would be expected that they be actively involved in the work of the congregation where they worship. The epistle is addressed to the "saints who are in Ephesus, and faithful in Christ Jesus" (Ephesians 1:1), not just to the men of the Ephesian church.

Now let's examine the Scriptures where we find that Paul meets Acquila and his wife Priscilla in Corinth. They had left Rome because Claudius had commanded all Jews to leave the city of Rome (Acts 18:1-2). Apparently Paul established a close relationship with this couple because they were involved in the same trade—tent making (Acts 18:3)—in addition to being believers in Jesus Christ. When Paul left for Syria, Acquila and Priscilla accompanied him (Acts 18:18). When they eventually arrived in Ephesus, they heard Apollos teaching the baptism of John so they, Acquila and Priscilla, took him aside and instructed him "the way of the God more accurately" (Acts 18:26) and we then find Apollos "showing from the Scriptures that Jesus is the Christ" (Acts 18:28). Who did the teaching to correct the error of Apollos' teaching? Acquilla and Priscilla. Why did Paul not command Priscilla to remain silent in this situation?

I have a very good friend who is an older woman and who is always ready to proclaim the gospel to those that she comes in contact with. One time she was teaching another lady in the lady's home and her husband was within hearing and became inquisitive about some of the passages they were discussing in the Bible, so my friend began to teach him as well as his wife. After some time both of them grew in faith in Jesus Christ and wanted to confess Christ and to repent and to become members of the church. When this lady teacher approached the preacher of the congregation (it did not have elders) where she worshipped about baptizing them, he publicly chastised her in the next worship service for teaching a man. She was very hurt by this action but she remained strong in her faith and commitment to carry out the Great Commission (Matthew 28:18-20). What is wrong with this picture when examined in light of the Great Commission? Aren't we all commanded to go forth and teach and baptize and to teach those that are converted the things that we have learned from the Scriptures? We are not commanded that men should teach men and women should teach women. I thank God for my friend's strength to continue to teach God's Word as the opportunity presented itself; she could have quit teaching altogether because of her treatment!

Now let's examine Acts 16:11-15:

> Therefore, sailing from Troas, we ran a straight course to Samothrace, and the next *day* came to Neapolis, and from there to Philippi, which is the foremost city of that part of Macedonia, a colony. And we were staying in that city for some days. And on the Sabbath day we went out of the city to the riverside, where prayer was customarily made; and we sat down and spoke to the women who met *there.* Now a certain woman named Lydia heard *us.* She was a seller of purple from the city of Thyatira, who worshiped God. The Lord opened her heart to heed the things spoken by Paul. And when she and her household were baptized, she begged *us,* saying, "If you have judged me to be faithful to the Lord, come to my house and stay." So she persuaded us.

What we find in this passage is when Paul journeyed to Philippi, he sought out a group to worship with on the following Sabbath. This group happened to be a group of women and they were apparently Jewish and engaged in prayer. Paul did not command them to be silent, instead he joined them in worship and taught them about Jesus, and Lydia's heart was opened to Paul's teachings and she and her household were baptized. We don't have Paul Harvey to give us the "rest of the story," but I can't imagine that these women remained silent. I can imagine that they engaged in converting others in accordance with God's Word for all Christians. The point I'm making is that the church at Philippi started with women and initially, at least, met in a woman's house.

We've looked at several passages of Scripture during the time of Christ on earth and several passages of Scripture written by Paul and other inspired writers. You can continue this study by looking at other passages of Scripture about women in the first century church if you desire. But in the interest of space, let's now look at those two Scriptures that appear to limit the role of women in the church.

First, I do not hold the position that women should be elders or deacons in the Lord's church because of the specific Scriptures about the "qualifications" of elders (pastors, shepherds, bishops) and deacons given in I Timothy 3:1-13 and in Titus 1:5-9 for these functions or ministries. I do hold the position that we should not limit God's Word when it comes to women's roles in the church of Christ.

Second, in view of all the recorded information about women in the New Testament, for someone to use two seemly obscure verses—when viewed in the context of the entire New Testament—to limit their role, especially when Paul does not do so in other passages of Scripture, seems to me to be a great disservice to our Christian women.

Let's look at the first passage of Scripture that some say limits the role of women in the church, I Corinthians 14: 34-35. It reads: "Let your women keep silent in the churches, for they are not permitted to speak; but *they are* to be submissive, as the law also says. And if they want to learn something, let them ask their own husbands at home; for it is shameful for women to speak in church." If we look at this verse as it reads, we can conclude that women are to be silent in the churches, but what if we look at it in the context of the book of I Corinthians where Paul writes of women praying in public? What if we look at it in the context of the New Testament?

Adam Clark (n.d.), in *Adam Clarke's Commentary on the New Testament,* aptly describes this passage of Scripture, and it is the same view I realized when looking at it through the lens of organization development in the context of the entire New Testament:

> Let your women keep silence in the churches—This was a Jewish ordinance; women were not permitted to teach in the assemblies, or even to ask questions. The rabbins taught that "a woman should know nothing but the use of her distaff." And the sayings of Rabbi Eliezer, as delivered, Bammidbar Rabba, sec. 9, fol. 204, are both worthy of remark and of execration; they are these: *yisrephu dibrey torah veal yimsaru lenashim*, "Let the words of the law

be burned, rather than that they should be delivered to women." This was their condition till the time of the Gospel, when, according to the prediction of Joel, the Spirit of God was to be poured out on the women as well as the men, that they might prophesy, i.e. teach. [Joel 2:28-29]. And that they did prophesy or teach is evident from what the apostle says, 1 Corinthians 11:5, where he lays down rules to regulate this part of their conduct while ministering in the church. (Clark, n. d., Electronic Version)

But does not what the apostle says here contradict that statement, and show that the words in chap. 11 should be understood in another sense? For, here it is expressly said that they should keep silence in the church; for it was not permitted to a woman to speak. Both places seem perfectly consistent. It is evident from the context that the apostle refers here to asking questions, and what we call dictating in the assemblies. It was permitted to any man to ask questions, to object, altercate, attempt to refute, etc., in the synagogue; but this liberty was not allowed to any woman. St. Paul confirms this in reference also to the Christian Church; he orders them to keep silence; and, if they wished to learn any thing, let them inquire of their husbands at home; because it was perfectly indecorous for women to be contending with men in public assemblies, on points of doctrine, cases of conscience, etc. But this by no means intimated that when a woman received any particular influence from God to enable her to teach, that she was not to obey that influence; on the contrary, she was to obey it, and the apostle lays down directions in chap. 11 for regulating her personal appearance when thus employed. All that the apostle opposes here is their questioning, finding fault, disputing, etc., in the Christian Church, as the Jewish men were permitted to do in their synagogues; together with the attempts to usurp any authority over the man, by setting up their judgment in opposition to them; for the apostle has in view, especially, acts of disobedience, arrogance, etc., of which no woman

> would be guilty who was under the influence of the Spirit of God. (Clark, n. d., Electronic Version)

I concur with the words of Adam Clark based on what my examination of the Scriptures revealed. We should also consider that the Greek word "silent" in verse 34 is *sigao*. According to Strong's Hebrew and Greek Dictionary it means to hush, indicating a temporary condition. We know that Paul is addressing several issues in the church at Corinth where some need to simply hush: it is the same word used in verses 28 and 30 about prophesying and speaking in tongues in the public services.

The next passage we examined that appears to some to limit the role of women or that women "usurp the authority of men" is I Timothy 2:11-14. "Let a woman learn in silence with all submission. And I do not permit a woman to teach or to have authority over a man, but to be in silence. For Adam was formed first, then Eve. And Adam was not deceived, but the woman being deceived, fell into transgression."

My understanding on silence here has already been stated in the discussion above so we will simply discuss the "usurping of authority." Lipscomb (1976) simply states, "The point guarded against here is woman's assuming authority over man. It is not wrong for her to teach the word of God, but wrong for her to teach it in a way that assumes authority or superiority over man. (Titus 2:5.) This is the only reason given in the Scriptures why it is wrong" (p. 143).

Again, when viewed in the context of the entire New Testament, these two passages appear to be relatively minor in importance, but much is made of them in some religious groups. Women were apparently publicly praying and prophesying in the church of Christ (I Corinthians 11:5) in the first century. This had been foretold when the prophet Joel wrote:

> And it shall come to pass afterward
> That I will pour out My Spirit on all flesh;
> Your sons and your daughters shall prophesy,
> Your old men shall dream dreams,
> Your young men shall see visions. (Joel 2:28)

We also read that Philip, who was an evangelist in the first century church of Christ, had four daughters that prophesied in public (Acts 21:9). The New Testament or Covenant describes all Christians as priests, saints, and equal members in the body of Christ, each possessing different gifts or talents. There are, however, passages that limit the function of women from the ministry of elders/bishops and/or deacons. My conclusion from this study of a woman's role in the church of Christ in the first century is that once again we have let the influence of the world invade our understanding of the Scriptures and the Lord's church to form a tradition that has corrupted the true understanding of the inspired Word of God.

An autonomous congregation of the Lord's church should listen to the spiritual oversight of its elders and rely on them to guide their spiritual well-being because they are after all responsible for the souls of the sheep that they shepherd. There are many differing views of the Scriptures and it is difficult to examine an issue that is so sensitive without drawing barbs from those that have opposing views. Paul wrote in Philippians 2:5 that we are to have the same mind as Jesus Christ, in other words, Christians are to be in unity with the teachings of Christ as we find them in the inspired Word. It appears from my examination of the New Testament that Christ Jesus did not hold any restricting views of women. In Chapter 4 of the same book we find:

> Finally, brethren, whatever things are true, whatever things *are* noble, whatever things *are* just, whatever things *are* pure, whatever things *are* lovely, whatever things *are* of good report, if *there is* any virtue and if *there is* anything praiseworthy—meditate on these things. The things which you learned and received and heard and saw in me, these do, and the God of peace will be with you. (Philippians 4:8-9)

I find the examples that Jesus used when dealing with women and using women in his teaching to be in concert with the majority of Paul's writings. Paul used some "limiting" words about women in these two passages we've reviewed and it is my observation that they are temporary solutions to temporary conditions and were used to teach those who were trying to follow Christ to do so in a more perfect way. Ferguson (1995) has examined many ancient writings from the first three centuries after the church came into being and concluded, "In orthodox mainstream circles the same situation prevailed as that reflected in the New Testament documents: a very full involvement of women in every aspect of the church's life except speaking in public liturgical assemblies and serving as elders/bishops" (p. 235).

Women went with Christ on his last journey from Galilee to Jerusalem (Matt. 25:55f; Mark 15:40f; Luke 23:49). They accompanied the persons carrying his body to the sepulcher (Matt. 27:61; Mark 15:47; Luke 23: 55) and the women prepared his body for burial (Luke 23:56). Women were the first to go to his tomb on the morning of the resurrection (Matthew 28:1; Mark 16:1; Luke 24:1; John 20:1) and the women were the first persons to whom the risen Christ revealed himself (Matthew 28:9, Mark 16:9; John 20:14). It was also women who first told his followers of the resurrection (Luke 24:9f, 22). Why would I want to restrict the work and service or functions of women in the church, other than from those functions of elders/bishops and/or deacons if Christ himself does not appear to do so?

One cannot dispute that there is the universal church and there are congregations of the church scattered wherever believers gather to worship our God. In those congregations, the members collectively must decide what the role and/or function of women in their respective congregations will be or will not be. The elders should oversee that decision-making process, with the involvement of the entire congregation, teaching and guiding the congregation according to the scriptural context of the topic of women's role in the church.

Now comes the "However." However; remember God's relationship to the children of Israel? It was that of a husband (Jeremiah 31:31-34). Remember Jesus' relationship to the church? It is that of a bridegroom or husband (John 3:29). Remember the family relationship of the husband and wife? (Matthew 19:5-6; I Corinthians 7; Ephesians 5:22-33; Colossians 3:18-19; I Peter 3:1-7). It is all about relationship and God's order of things. In today's world, many men have relegated their role in the family to the wife. In many modern congregations of the lord's church the role of elders and deacons have been relegated to women.

I do not present here an argument that the role of modern women should be expanded beyond that of the first century, but I'm afraid that this is another case where we see more evidence of the influence of the world on women's roles in the church than we see the influence of the Scriptures. We must return to the Holy Scriptures to see what it teaches and that return to the Scriptures must be under the oversight of good shepherds, and not be influenced by conventions/seminars where it is advocated that women serve in roles expressly set aside as a function delegated to men. I certainly don't know God's mind in this matter and the "why" of the structure put forth in his Word but it is a matter that must be openly discussed and taught.

Remember Jesus expressly said, "If you love me, keep my commandments" (John 14:15).

Our women do valuable services in our congregations and I sincerely believe that they should be recognized for it. They are a part of the church and they have special gifts that men do not ordinarily possess. I believe that we are afraid to recognize the work and efforts of women because we are afraid of the criticism of other congregations that are buried in traditions that may not be in accord with God's Word.

Chapter 11
Followers of Christ

"... And the disciples were first called Christians in Antioch" Acts 11:26).

Zig Ziglar (2000) told the following story about two men who worked for the railroad. On an extremely hot day, a crew of men was working on the road bed of the railroad when they were interrupted by a very slow moving train. The train came to a stop and a window in the last car—which incidentally was custom made and air conditioned—was raised. A booming, friendly voice called out, "Dave is that you?"

Dave Anderson, the crew chief called back, "Sure is, Jim, and it's really good to see you."

With that pleasant exchange, Dave Anderson was invited to join Jim Murphy, the president of the railroad, for a visit. For over an hour the men exchanged pleasantries and then shook hands warmly as the train pulled out.

Dave Anderson's crew immediately surrounded him and to a man expressed astonishment that he knew Jim Murphy, the president of the railroad, as a personal friend. Dave then explained that over twenty years earlier he and Jim had started to work for the railroad on the same day. One of the men, half-jokingly and half-seriously, asked Dave why he was still working out in the hot sun and Jim Murphy had gotten to be president. Rather wistfully, Dave explained, "Twenty-three years ago I went to work for $1.75 an hour and Jim Murphy went to work for the railroad" (Ziglar, 2000).

Why do I repeat this story—because I want to use it to make a point by looking at a different perspective? Dave Anderson became an employee of the railroad for the benefits while Jim Murphy became a part of the railroad. I want you to consider this question, "When you accepted Christ as your Savior, were baptized, and added to the saved, did you become a part of the church or did you just want the benefits?" The church is an organism and all its parts are needed and they are needed to do the function that their spiritual gifts lead them to do. Being a Christian is not a spectator sport!

This chapter is about followers and followership. We need to understand what a follower is. Webster says a follower is one in the service of another; one that follows the opinions or teachings of another: a *disciple*; one that imitates another. As followers or disciples of Jesus Christ, we are to imitate him to the best of our talents or spiritual gifts.

Paul, in his letter to the Ephesians, reminded them that they are the church and that it was built on the foundation of the apostles and prophets with Christ as the cornerstone. He emphasizes that they, as Christians, are the dwelling place of God in the Spirit (Ephesians 2:19-22). Peter also reminded believers that Jesus was the cornerstone and the fulfillment of the prophets and that Christians are the "spiritual house, a royal priesthood," and are to "offer up spiritual sacrifices acceptable to God through Jesus Christ" (I peter 2:4-8).

Luke tells us in Acts 11:25-26 "Then Barnabas departed for Tarsus to seek Saul. And when he had found him, he brought him to Antioch. So it was that for a whole year they assembled with the church and taught a great many people. And the disciples were first called Christians in Antioch." Now this Scripture begs the question, "Why were they called Christians?" It was foretold (Isaiah 62:2) and these first century Christians were seen as followers or disciples of Jesus Christ.

Barnabas and Paul were in Antioch for a year and during that time they taught a great many people. It is quite evident that there must have been a significant enough change brought about by Barnabas' and Paul's teachings that others saw they followed the teachings of Christ so they began to call them Christians because they followed Christ's teachings and imitated Christ. So we find then that Christians were soon recognized as followers or disciples of Christ.

A person after hearing the Good News is, through his or her faith, baptized and added to the church of Christ. This is the universal church of Christ. The church depicted in the New Testament and the one in need of restoration to that first century model. A person makes a covenant or psychological contract to associate themselves with a congregation of believers and this is most often the congregation in which one confessed Christ and was consequently baptized. A covenant is a binding agreement between the individual and Christ. A psychological contract is "an individual's belief regarding the terms and conditions of a reciprocal exchange agreement between that person and another person" (Rousseau, 1989). That person has then become a follower of Christ, his disciple. When one has obeyed the gospel and been added to the church, he is a child of God through his faith in Jesus Christ. Most of us do not reflect deeply enough about the covenant or psychological contract we make with Jesus Christ.

> For you are all sons of God through faith in Christ Jesus. For as many of you as were baptized into Christ have put on Christ. There is neither Jew nor Greek, there is neither slave nor free, there is neither male nor female; for you are all one in Christ Jesus. And if you *are* Christ's, then you are Abraham's seed, and heirs according to the promise. (Galatians 3:26-29)

Today leaders in the church are faced with many issues that they do not seem to be able to get their hands around. There are demands for change. First, contemporary society has changed dramatically over the last few decades in that everything is about change and some members of the church of Christ want to bring change into the church. In order to grow numerically, some groups are bringing drastic change into various Christian groups to appeal to the masses without regard to what is written in the inspired Scriptures.

Second, traditional views of the family have changed in the societies of today. There is generational and gender segmentation. The church leaders take great risk if they ignore the generation gaps within their respective congregations. Younger people are not looking for the same things that the old silent majority is looking for in the church of Christ. We have the "silent majority," the "boomers," the "X-generation," and the "Y-generation" and they all have different needs and expectations. Congregational leaders also need to be publicly addressing the gender segmentation by teaching what the Scriptures tell us about these gender issues. Yes, I'm writing about homosexuality as well as the acceptance of same-sex couples in some churches. I'm also talking about different-sex people living together without the benefit of marriage—another institution of God that is just as important as the institution of the church. Paul compares the marriage of husband and wife to the church and its relationship to Christ in Ephesians 5:23-32. We also have couples having babies out of wedlock. This is a clear indication that fornication has occurred but they are often accepted in the church without ever confessing their sins. When they are singled out, the majority of the time the girl has to endure the brunt of any stigma that occurs while the boy goes on with his life.

Next, women's roles in the church are also in question in many people's minds. This mindset is influenced by societal shifts in women's roles in the workplace and in the home. These societal shifts are publicized in the media and more often than not they cast aspersions on the institution of marriage. It is time for church leaders to address this issue about women's roles but only with a clear understanding of what the Scriptures reveal about it.

And finally, church leaders are in a dilemma about membership that does not get involved. There are many reasons for this. One of them is that we have institutionalized the church. We hire men to do the preaching. We select elders to oversee the flock and it seems that every member has a different view of what that encompasses. We appoint deacons to do the work of the church and then we do not support them. We get teachers to teach our children and to teach us and we sit back and complain about what they're teaching, how they're teaching, and why our children are leaving the church in droves.

Followership is about getting involved with the work of the church under the oversight of the elders and carried out by the deacons or other ministry leaders. Leaders need excellent followers and together they constitute a team that accomplishes the mission of the organization. Christians should not just sit quietly and just accept whatever decisions the congregational leaders are making without voicing their concern if the congregation is moving away from what the Scriptures teach us. We are disciples of Christ and as such, we need to protect the Word and make sure that we know its contents. Peter describes some of the characteristics of followers of Christ:

> Likewise you younger people, submit yourselves to *your* elders. Yes, all of *you* be submissive to one another, and be clothed with humility, for *"God resists the proud, But gives grace to the humble."*
>
> Therefore humble yourselves under the mighty hand of God, that He may exalt you in due time, casting all

> your care upon Him, for He cares for you. Be sober, be vigilant; because your adversary the devil walks about like a roaring lion, seeking whom he may devour. Resist him, steadfast in the faith, knowing that the same sufferings are experienced by your brotherhood in the world. But may the God of all grace, who called us to His eternal glory by Christ Jesus, after you have suffered a while, perfect, establish, strengthen, and settle *you.* (I Peter 5:5-10)

This chapter can't solve the dilemma facing church leaders and their efforts to get all their members involved in the work of the church of Christ, but it can exhort the readers to go back to the Scriptures and see what it says about Jesus, the church, and his followers. We know what happened in the church of the first century. It's recorded in the book of Acts and the epistles that follow. As a personal outcome of this reading, lay a foundation for yourself so that you will continue to study the Scriptures and find for yourself what you should be doing as a Christian. Become a modern era Berean (Acts 17:10-11)! Restore the church to its initial structure, the organism, so that through unity and single purpose it can grow as it is God's will.

Having written all this as a lead-in to this chapter I posit this question. Do members of the church of Christ understand their role as follower of Christ? I think not in many cases. I see too many evidences of the secular world in the church of Christ. As members of the church, each generation must "search the Scriptures daily to find out whether these things were so" (Acts 17:11). That was their culture in the first century and it should be the culture in the church today. Consider this book as a help in searching the Scriptures and bringing you and every other member back to the same intensity exhibited by the first century converts, but do not take this book as truth. Examine whether the things I write are according to God's Word. "And they continued steadfastly in the apostles' doctrine and fellowship, in the breaking of bread, and in prayers" (Acts 2:42). As we examine this lesson on followers let's follow God's own words, "Come now, and let us reason together" (Isaiah1:18) about what WE should be doing.

Now, let's go back to the initial question. "When you accepted Christ as your Savior, were baptized, and added to the church, did you become a part of the church or did you just want the benefits?" The answer you discern about yourself is very important as a follower of Christ. Paul tells the Colossians "And whatever you do, do it heartily, as to the Lord and not to men, knowing that from the Lord you will receive the reward of the inheritance; for you serve the Lord Christ" (Colossians 3:23-24). Paul's words to the Colossians are applicable to Christians today. This inheritance is heaven—that is why we should know what is expected of us as followers of Christ.

I am not implying that we can work our way into salvation like Dave and Jim, in the above story of the railroad, worked their way into the railroad, albeit with different intentions. Jesus' brother addresses this issue of work for us. He wrote, "But be doers of the word, and not hearers only, deceiving yourselves" (James 1:22) and "But do you want to know, O foolish man, that faith without works is dead" (James 2:20). Again, this is another lesson and now we need to focus on what you and I are supposed to do as followers of Jesus Christ. Again, being a Christian is not a spectator sport. Jesus said, "If you love me, you keep my commandments" (John 14:15).

In his latter days here on earth, Jesus was teaching his disciples, the twelve he had selected to lead the establishment of his church, and was preparing them for his departure (John 13 and 14). He had washed their feet and explained to them that this was an example of serving one another. They should be servant leaders first. He told them of the betrayer in their midst. He foretold Peter's denial of him on that last night and morning before his trial. He comforted them and said he was going to prepare a place for them and he answered questions from Thomas, Phillip, and Judas (not Iscariot). There were then and are today many lessons in the discourse of these two chapters but two that I think today's followers of Christ need to reflect on as a foundation for examining themselves and where they are in God's kingdom.

In John 13: 34-35, Jesus told his disciples, "A new commandment I give to you, that you love one another; as I have loved you, that you also love one another. By this all will know that you are My disciples, if you love one another." And then he reminded them in John 14:15, "If you love me, keep my commandments" (John 14:15). I find it very impacting that Jesus emphasized these two Christian principles during this last time with his eleven disciples (Judas Iscariot had left the Passover Feast and his replacement had not been selected.). We are to love one another as Jesus loves us to the extent that the world sees that love in us. We are to keep Jesus' commandments if we love him! We will look at some additional Scriptures that add to what Christians are to do.

And you might say, "Oh, but he was talking to his eleven disciples."

And I say, "That is very true but later he says that these eleven disciples are to teach others to do whatsoever he taught them and so on and so on right up to this present day."

And you say, "Where did Jesus say this?"

He said it in Matthew 28: 19-20. "Go therefore and make disciples of all the nations, baptizing them in the name of the Father and of the Son and of the Holy Spirit, teaching them to observe all things that I have commanded you; and lo, I am with you always, even to the end of the age."

Well, we now have several things that we are supposed to do as Christians: be servant leaders, love one another so that the world sees this love, keep the commandments of Jesus, and go out and teach people the good news, baptize them, and teach them to teach others to do whatever Jesus commanded the original disciples to do. In order to do these things we have to be engaged in examining and discovering the lessons for Christians in God's Word.

God also expects us to be faithful (I Corinthians 4:2). He expects us to be ourselves and use what we have (Matthew 25: 14-28). He expects us to stay true to him as he is true to us (John 14:1-3). He expects us to be stewards, or better translated "house servants," who use their power under the authority of the house owner—in other words we are empowered to carry out the duties of the church of the Lord (I Corinthians 4:1-3). This is in reference to the church and the Christians in the church. We are authorized to teach and preach and baptize those that hear the Word, have faith, and proclaim Jesus Christ as their Lord and Savior before other men.

Are you keeping count? Christians now have many things to do—be servants, love one another so that the world sees this love, keep the commandments of Jesus, and go out and teach people the good news, baptize them, and teach them to teach others to do whatever Jesus commanded the original disciples to do, and keep our faith.

God wants us to have a mind like that of Jesus "Let this mind be in you which was also in Christ Jesus" (Philippians 2:5). Peter wrote that Christians are to be of the same mind (I Peter 4:1). Now, logic says that if Christians are to have a like mind to that of Jesus and they're to be of the same mind with other Christians, why do we have so much conflict and trouble between members of the church? I do not have the answer to this very troubling question but I suspect it's because our level of commitment to Jesus and to his church is weak. Satan is pulling on the strings of our lusts and those lusts lead us to sin. It's just easier to go with the ways of the world and with tradition instead of daily searching the Scriptures for truth and encouragement.

A careful reading of John 17 reveals that Jesus spent some of his last time here on earth as a man praying for me and for you. Do you know that Jesus has prayed for you and what that should mean to each one of us who profess to be Christians? He prayed for those disciples that would become apostles and then he began to pray for me and to pray for you. These are his words when he prayed for us:

> I do not pray for these alone, but also for those who will believe in Me through their word; that they all may be one, as You, Father, *are* in Me, and I in You; that they also may be one in Us, that the world may believe that You sent Me. And the glory which You gave Me I have given them, that they may be one just as We are one: I in them, and You in Me; that they may be made perfect in one, and that the world may know that You have sent Me, and have loved them as You have loved Me. (John 17:20-23)

Jesus wants us to be unified in him and his Father and in each other. Where does that leave room for all these different Christian religious groups? How can we be one if we're following different conventions and doctrines and in some cases, ungodly men and women? The answer to that is that we can't be one until we are of a like mind with each other and Jesus and God the Father. We do that by studying his Word and then following his Word. There is no other way.

Today's followers of Christ should recognize and esteem the elders or shepherds that labor among us. Their function is to keep us scriptural and to admonish us when we stray from the Word in order that our souls may be saved. We should be prompt in taking mundane tasks away from the elders because our souls are important, and they are charged, as part of their function in the organism, to keep us safe from the evil one—to look after our souls. All Christians are to be at peace with one another. We are to "comfort the fainthearted, uphold the weak, be patient with all." We are to see that no one does evil to others and we are to pursue good for ourselves as well as others. We are to "rejoice always, pray without ceasing, in everything give thanks;" for it is God's will that we do these things. The inspired Word says that we should not "quench the Spirit." We are not to despise the prophecies, but to hold fast to the Word for it is good, and we are to stay away from any form of evil (I Thessalonians 5:12-22).

Peter writes of Christians as stewards of the manifold grace of God (I Peter 4:7-11). We are to be serious and to pray, but above all we need to have fervent love for each other as well as be hospitable without complaining. I can't believe my ears when I hear some Christian complain about helping someone in a time of difficulty. I just want to scream, "Well, why did you do it if you can't do whatever it is you're doing in love because of the grace that God has for us?" Whatever we do, it should be to glorify God through Jesus Christ (II Timothy 2).

All Christians have some gift from God, and as followers we are to use those gifts to work together for the good of the church (Romans 12:4-8). Again, Paul refers to the church as an organism or body, but we do not all have the same function. We each provide a function to the congregation of the Lord according to our gift. Remember, this is not a spectator sport; it is the church and we are all to do whatever we need to do in order that the seed of the gospel will be spread. We do not have to worry about growth, God will take care of that; we only need to sow the seed.

In order to keep harmony or unity in the church, we are to follow Jesus' teachings. Go in love to the one who faults you or sins against you and work out the differences. We often go to the elders or the preacher but we do not go to the one we should go to—the one who sins against us (Matthew 18:15-17). It has been said:

- The *wrong words* said at the *wrong time* discourage me.
- The *wrong words* said at the *right time* frustrate me.
- The *right words* said at the *wrong time* confuse me.
- The *right words* said at the *right time* encourage me. (Maxwell & Parrott, 2005, p. 47)

Would it not be great if we all said, and meant, the words of Jeremiah, "As for me and my house, we will serve the Lord" (Jeremiah 29:11).

Remember if we're going to have traditions, let them be the traditions of the Scriptures (I Corinthians 11:2).

One parting thought:

"Sow a thought,
Reap a deed.
Sow a deed,
Reap a habit.
Sow a habit,
Reap a destiny." (Unknown)

Additional Readings for Followers

There are many other Scriptures that tell us, as Christians, as followers of Christ, what we are to be about. Following is a small sample for your continued study:

- Christians are the temple of God (I Corinthians 3:16) and Jesus is the foundation of the church (I Corinthians 3:11) but Christians need to build on the foundation as Paul so aptly told us (I Corinthians 3:10-11).
- As we saw in chapter two, Christians are the church—the called out. The church is a spiritual building, our body. It is not a building of mortar, brick, and timber. Buildings of sticks and bricks are simply a convenient place for the church (Christians) to come together to worship and fellowship.
- We have to work out our own salvation (Philippians 2:12) but it must be in the context of Jesus' Word as given to us in the New Testament.
- John 14:15 "If you love me, keep my commandments."
- Hebrews 10:24 "Let us consider one another in order to stir up love and good works."
- A disciple of Jesus repents (Acts 17:30); abides in his Word (John 8:31-32); obeys him (John 14:15); teaches and baptizes others (Matthew 28:19); grows in grace and knowledge of our Lord and Savior Jesus Christ (II Peter 3:18); and exhibits patience and follows his steps (I Peter 2:21). We could continue this thought on and on to include many traits that a Christian should exhibit, but you get the drift.
- John the Baptist knew his place and he understood Jesus' role (John 3: 28-30). Shouldn't we do the same?
- We're issued a warning. There will be few who follow Jesus' way of life (Matthew 7:13-14). Don't you want to be one of the few?
- Christians went everywhere preaching the Word (Acts 8:1-4). Are we remiss today when we don't do the same?
- Servants of the Lord must not quarrel, be gentle to all, be able to teach, be patient, and correct those in opposition so that they may know the truth (II Timothy 2:24-25).
- Jesus is the high priest of the church of Christ (Hebrews 5) and the believers and followers of Jesus are a kingdom of priests (I Peter 2:5-9).

- "To me, who am less than the least of all the saints, this grace was given, that I should preach among the Gentiles the unsearchable riches of Christ, and to make all see what *is* the fellowship of the mystery, which from the beginning of the ages has been hidden in God who created all things through Jesus Christ; to the intent that now the manifold wisdom of God might be made known by the church to the principalities and powers in the heavenly *places,* according to the eternal purpose which He accomplished in Christ Jesus our Lord, in whom we have boldness and access with confidence through faith in Him" (Ephesians 3:8-12).
- Followers are to act/live (I Thessalonians 5:11-24).
- What are some of the things the Lord's people are called? Saints (Romans 1:6-7; 8:28); children of God (Romans 8:16); faithful in Christ (Ephesians 1:1); elect (I Peter 1:1); Sons of God (Romans 8:14); servants of Christ (Philippians 1:1); Christians (Acts 11:26).
- Christians are to offer spiritual sacrifices of praise and thanksgiving (Hebrews 13:15; I Peter 2:5).
- A Christian's motivation (II Corinthians 4: 16-18).
- Holy living guidelines (I Thessalonians 5).
- Be filled with the spirit (Ephesians 5:18-21).
- We should desire to be sent when needed (Isaiah 6:8). Do you participate in mission work in some way?
- It is a Christian's responsibility to show Jesus' glory in the church (Ephesians 3:19-21). Do those you associate with outside the congregation know that you are a Christian?
- Boldness is a characteristic of Jesus' followers (Acts 4:13; 18-20; 29; 31). Are you bold in carrying the gospel to others?
- Romans 12:2 is one of the guiding Scriptures for studying God's Word. Are worldly things more important to you than the church?
- "The kingdom of God is within you" (Luke 17:21).Christians are God's field and building (I Corinthians 3:6-9). Do you keep it holy?
- It is the responsibility of followers that they must know the elders (I Thessalonians 5:12).

- Teaching is to be done by all believers (I Corinthians 14: 26, 31) in some way, not just those who received the gift of teaching from the Holy Spirit (Ephesians 4:11; James 3:1).
- God desires that all should be saved (I Timothy 2:3-4).
- Jesus is the high priest of the church of Christ (Hebrews 5) and the believers and followers of Jesus are a kingdom of priests (I Peter 2:5-9).
- Be sexually moral (I Thessalonians 4:3-5).

Chapter 12
Servant Leadership: Jesus' Model

"Let this mind be in you which was also in Christ Jesus, who, being in the form of God, did not consider it robbery to be equal with God, but made Himself of no reputation, taking the form of a bondservant, and coming in the likeness of men. And being found in appearance as a man, He humbled Himself and became obedient to the point of death, even the death of the cross"
(Philippians 2:5-8).

As we examine secular leaders that we come in contact with on a regular basis we see many different leadership styles: autocratic, participative, charismatic, transformational, servant leaders, and so forth. Any of these leadership styles may be appropriate as well as practiced in various situations in the secular world and in the Christian world. This study will focus on only one of those styles—servant leadership—because religious leaders should all exhibit servant leadership as their prevalent or dominant leadership style. Certain situations may dictate another leadership on a temporary basis. In the secular world the terminology "servant leadership" is attributed to Robert K. Greenleaf from his seminal 1970 essay "The Servant as Leader." His concept of the servant as leader came from his reading of Hermann Hesse's "Journey to the East" and his concepts of servant leadership are widely read, widely accepted, and practiced in many areas of the secular world. While some of the concepts of Greenleaf's servant leader are consistent with Jesus' teachings of servant leadership, there are differences and if we see Greenleaf's servant leadership practiced in some organizations in the secular world, we might easily think they are consistent with Jesus' teachings. However; Christians should want to only practice servant leadership in the church and in the world that is consistent with what Jesus taught his disciples.

Dubrin (2007) defines a servant leader as one who "serves constituents by working on their behalf to help them achieve their goals, not the leader's own goals" (p. 111). He further states that the key aspects of servant leadership are: "place service before self-interest; listen first to express confidence in others; inspire trust by being trustworthy; focus on what is feasible to accomplish; and lend a hand" (p. 111).

Warren Bennis tells us that "The most dangerous leadership myth is that leaders are born—that there is a genetic factor to leadership. This myth asserts that people simply either have certain charismatic qualities or not. That's nonsense; in fact, the opposite is true. Leaders are made rather than born" (as cited in Hunter, 2004, p. 42).

Jesus gives us a very clear example of this in that he spent three years developing his twelve disciples, eleven of which became apostles, before the church was established. It's clear to me that people make a psychological contract whenever they enter into any phase of their life whether it is as a parent, husband or wife, coach, teacher, minister, or employee. In doing so we become servant leaders because we're going to take responsibility for our action in that role and in all of the roles serve others. When people change into better leaders or decide that they need to lead others to Christ, most will tell you it is because they decided to change.

This study will examine servant leadership from that older source—the New Testament of the Bible. Servant leadership should develop with one's understanding of himself or herself as a disciple of Christ, but we don't always develop into servant leaders because our understanding of our role is clouded by traditions and worldly experiences. We bring the leadership paradigms of the world and the leadership training we receive in the world into the "leadership" roles in the Lord's church. Those paradigms and training are shaped by leadership structures that we see in the military, businesses, governments, and other organizations. The leaders are always at the top of the hierarchy of the organization or in positions of power so we bring these sad old paradigms with us when we come into God's kingdom, the church of Christ. Jesus didn't intend it to be this way and this concept must be a major shift in thinking for many who are in leadership roles in the church today. The reason is that the infiltration of worldly leadership styles and organizational structure into the church has occurred over a very long time. I have surveyed many people from many different Christian groups, and over 80% of the time when asked to depict the church, they do so in a hierarchical manner.

According to Moffatt (1938), toward the end of the first century, after the establishment of the church, a "mono-episcopate" [lead elder] began to emerge out of the presbyters [eldership]. There is not a clear reason for this phenomenon which started in Syria and Asia Minor. As this leadership model developed, there emerged a bishop over the eldership, and deacons or assistants became the third tier of congregational ministry. This practice was common during the time of Ignatius but there were no such leadership practices in Philippi, Corinth, or Rome until later (p. 44-45).

Regardless of the leadership role a man or woman plays in the church, it must not supersede Jesus' headship or supplant his power and authority. Jesus alone is the head of the church and his leadership style alone should be the example that all Christians follow in their various functions as Christians or followers of Christ.

Jesus told his disciples, "If you love me, keep my commandments" (John 14:15). I remind you of this saying by Jesus because we will see in the following Scriptures several titles that we should not use in addressing religious leaders and we will also see how Jesus describes servant leaders. Christians should not serve for the sake of the title or position. Jesus was very clear about servant leaders and how they are to be addressed.

> Then Jesus spoke to the multitudes and to his disciples, saying: "The scribes and the Pharisees sit in Moses' seat. Therefore whatever they tell you to observe, *that* observe and do, but do not do according to their works; for they say, and do not do. For they bind heavy burdens, hard to bear, and lay *them* on men's shoulders; but they *themselves* will not move them with one of their fingers. But all their works they do to be seen by men. They make their phylacteries[2] broad and enlarge the borders of their garments. They love the best places at feasts, the best seats in the synagogues, greetings

2 **phy·lac·ter·ies**. **1.** *Judaism.* Either of two small leather boxes, each containing strips of parchment inscribed with quotations from the Hebrew Scriptures, one of which is strapped to the forehead and the other to the left arm by Orthodox and Conservative Jewish men during morning worship, except on the Sabbath and holidays.

> in the marketplaces, and to be called by men, 'Rabbi, Rabbi.' But you, do not be called 'Rabbi'; for One is your Teacher, the Christ, and you are all brethren. Do not call anyone on earth your father; for One is your Father, He who is in heaven. And do not be called teachers; for One is your Teacher, the Christ. But he who is greatest among you shall be your servant. And whoever exalts himself will be humbled, and he who humbles himself will be exalted. (Matthew 23:1-12)

Moffatt (1938) had this to say about "titles" in his study of the early church during the first five centuries:

> ... the faithful continued to refuse the title of 'Lord' to anyone except Jesus Christ, who alone was to establish the divine Order [church] upon earth. It was their way of upholding what he stood for, at all costs, and they would not yield to any compromise in this issue any more than to subtler attempts in the direction of fusing their faith with non-political syncretistic movements of the ages. (p. 42)

Even though we have assigned the title of minister to those that preach God's Word; elder, shepherd, bishop, or pastor to those that have spiritual responsibilities in the congregation; or deacon to those that head up special programs or departments of a congregation of the Lord's church, these titles are descriptive of a role in the congregation, not a title to exalt those in these roles above other Christians. They are not offices or positions. Any Christian can be a minister if they have the talents needed in the ministry, they can function in the role of an elder or deacon if they exhibit the qualities of these roles as described in the Scriptures. All Christians are ministers if they are doing God's will as they serve the needs of those around them. All Christians are disciples (followers of Christ) and all disciples are ministers and all ministers should be servant leaders. There are none above the other (I Corinthians 12:12-26). The elders or deacons or evangelists or any other "office holders" in the church are not above the members of a congregation of the Lord's church, they are *among* the members of the Lord's church, but they are performing a specific role or function. For example, the elders' or shepherd's function is to serve the church of Christ and the member in it by overseeing their spiritual welfare.

We need to draw on our understanding of leadership in the church through the concepts of the New Testament because with the establishment of the church, as recorded in the Book of Acts, the rules changed. The Old Testament is there for our learning the history of God's people and the various covenants of those times but the church was established and it is the last covenant of the Scriptures. Jesus used every opportunity to teach his disciples and those lessons he taught them are contained in the Scriptures for our learning as his disciples today. One of the lessons is in Matthew 20 as Jesus again addresses the need for Christians to be servant leaders. The mother of James and John approached Jesus and asked for favored positions for her sons. The other disciples became upset on hearing her request because they all desired those favored positions. This is the nature of man. Jesus, the greatest teacher ever, responded to them:

> You know that the rulers of the Gentiles lord it over them, and those who are great exercise authority over them. Yet it shall not be so among you; but whoever desires to become great among you, let him be your servant. And whoever desires to be first among you, let him be your slave—just as the Son of Man did not come to be served, but to serve, and to give His life a ransom for many. (Matthew 20:25-28)

Jesus took this opportunity to teach his disciples that while they may see autocratic leadership and positional leadership in the community, it is not a desired leadership style in his church. The leadership style of ministers or disciples of Christ is that of servant leader. His disciples are not leaders over others but they are servants among those they serve.

At another time and place Jesus again addressed the issue of position among his disciples. He compared those that truly lead in his kingdom as servants and added emphasis by teaching them that they should even receive little children as if they were him and his Father, our God.

> Then He came to Capernaum. And when He was in the house He asked them, "What was it you disputed among yourselves on the road?" But they kept silent, for on the road they had disputed among themselves who *would be the* greatest. And He sat down, called the twelve, and said to them, "If anyone desires to be first, he shall be last of all and servant of all." Then He took a little child and set him in the midst of them. And when He had taken

> him in His arms, He said to them, "Whoever receives one of these little children in My name receives Me; and whoever receives Me, receives not Me but Him who sent Me. (Mark 9:33-37)

The very foundation for servant leadership is agape love. In the following passage, Jesus is taking an opportunity to teach his disciples the reason they were chosen and the reason he was teaching or training them was so that they could be not only servants, but "fruit bearers."

> These things I have spoken to you, that My joy may remain in you, and *that* your joy may be full. This is My commandment, that you love one another as I have loved you. Greater love has no one than this, than to lay down one's life for his friends. You are My friends if you do whatever I command you. No longer do I call you servants, for a servant does not know what his master is doing; but I have called you friends, for all things that I heard from My Father I have made known to you. You did not choose Me, but I chose you and appointed you that you should go and bear fruit, and *that* your fruit should remain, that whatever you ask the Father in My name He may give you. These things I command you, that you love one another. (John 15:11-17)

They were to love Jesus as he had loved them and if they did they were his friends. Have you considered yourself to be Jesus' friend? You can be and you are if you are a Christian because these disciples were to teach those they converted the same lessons that Jesus taught them (Matthew 28:18-20). If we, as Christians, do the things that Jesus has taught us to do through the inspired Word, then we are servant leaders as well. I want to emphasize that all Christians are to act as servant leaders the majority of the time. That is the dominate style of leadership that Jesus taught the disciples while he was here with them and that is what he teaches us today through his inspired Word. We are not to just accept him as our Savior and then sit back and wait for his second coming, we are to continue this cycle of converting others and teaching them. Again, Christianity is not a spectator sport! It is our responsibility as Christians to do all these things, but we have institutionalized the church by hiring preachers and hiring missionaries and selecting elders to serve the congregation and appointing deacons to lead by serving in the various ministries that the congregation is involved with while we just sit back and wait. We are building walls around the church that should not be there. The church has to be externally focused to evangelize others and internally focused only to be taught, to edify, to be benevolent, and to grow in Christ. We have to wake up and reexamine the Scriptures and study and understand that Jesus intended that all his followers be servant leaders and teachers. I realize that we all have different gifts or talents, but one thing I know from observing members of the Lord's church is that we all might have gifts and talents, but we simply do not use them as we are taught in his Word (Matthew 25:14-26; I Corinthians 12:1-11; Romans 12:6-8).

As servants of Christ, and I contend all Christians are servant leaders of Christ, we have to be faithful. Our faith means that we have to believe in Jesus Christ and act on that belief. It is not good enough to just have believed or to have faith, but that belief requires action. Why? Even the demons believed in God—and they trembled because of that belief (James 2:18-24). James also tells us in this short passage that faith without works is what? Dead! Faith and works go hand-in-hand. Paul wrote to the Corinthians that faithfulness is required of servants of Christ and stewards of the mysteries of God—His Word. We just need to do what Christians need to do and God will judge and praise us when the time comes for judging and praising.

> Let a man so consider us, as servants of Christ and stewards of the mysteries of God. Moreover it is required in stewards that one be found faithful. But with me it is a very small thing that I should be judged by you or by a human court. In fact, I do not even judge myself. For I know of nothing against myself, yet I am not justified by this; but He who judges me is the Lord. Therefore judge nothing before the time, until the Lord comes, who will both bring to light the hidden things of darkness and reveal the counsels of the hearts. Then each one's praise will come from God. (I Corinthians 4:1-5)

In the work place or any other environment in which a Christian finds himself or herself, he or she should set the best example possible and demonstrate submissiveness, patience, and follow in the footsteps of Christ as his servants. Peter writes:

> Servants, *be* submissive to *your* masters with all fear, not only to the good and gentle, but also to the harsh. For

> this *is* commendable, if because of conscience toward God one endures grief, suffering wrongfully. For what credit *is it* if, when you are beaten for your faults, you take it patiently? But when you do good and suffer, if you take it patiently, this *is* commendable before God. For to this you were called, because Christ also suffered for us, leaving us an example, that you should follow His steps: (I Peter 2:18-21)

Jesus used the parable of the Good Samaritan (Luke 10:30-35) to teach that Christian servant leaders should all give and serve others because of compassion. The wounded man was passed by the priest without the priest offering any assistance. A Levite also came along and passed by the wounded man by moving to the other side of the road. Then along comes the Samaritan who was hated and despised by the Jews of that day. He stopped and did what he could to help the injured man and then took him to the inn where he arranged for further aid. This Samaritan demonstrated not only compassion but is the example of a servant leader that Jesus wants all of us to be. When the Samaritan saw a need, he took action to see that the need was satisfied.

Those first century Christians also demonstrated that they helped other congregations whenever there was a need (Acts 11:27-30). In the days of Claudius Caesar there would be a great famine throughout the whole world prophesied Agabus, so when it occurred the congregation gave as they had ability and sent the gift to the brethren in Judea. It was delivered to the elders by Barnabus and Saul.

In closing this chapter, I give you these questions to ask yourself so you can make your own determination as to whether you practice servant leadership in the church of our Lord and Savior:

- Do I **S**erve in a congregational ministry?
- How do I **E**valuate myself and my involvement in the congregation and its ministries?
- Is my ministry **R**elevant to the mission of the congregation and the church?
- Do I add **V**alue to the church, both physically and spiritually?
- Is my **A**ttitude based on positive Christian attributes?
- Do I **N**urture others and help them grow in God's Word?
- Do I **T**each others about the gospel at every opportunity?

Chapter 13
Congregational Planning

"Where there is no vision the people perish: …"
(Proverbs 29:18, KJV).

There is an old adage that reveals much truth – "A vision without a plan is just a dream. A plan without vision is just drudgery, but a vision with a plan can change the world." I don't know the origin of this adage but I do know from experience that it holds much truth. You might ask, "What does it have to do with the church of Christ? We have the Scriptures."

We indeed have the Scriptures and I want to present some of them to you through the lens of organization development as related to congregational planning. First, a couple of questions. "Do congregations of the Lord's church plan?" Some do and some don't and some do a little and some do a lot. The second question we need to ask ourselves is, "What is our reason for being?" If every member is not certain why the congregation is here, then we need a congregational planning and leadership development process that involves all the members of the congregation.

We are going to explore what the Scriptures teach about planning for the future of the church. First, let's look at some examples in the Old Testament. Proverbs 29:18 tells us, "Where *there is* no vision, the people perish: …" (KJV). The Psalmist tells us, "Unless the LORD builds the house, They labor in vain who build it; …" (Psalms 127:1).

If we examine the first seven chapters of Nehemiah, we find that he determined to rebuild the wall surrounding Jerusalem. His plans are laid out in the first seven chapters of that book. First of all, in chapter one we find that he prayed in preparation. He asked God's assistance in all aspects of what he planned to do. Next, we're told in chapter two, he took action and when the opportunity came, he presented his case to the very person who could provide approval for the resources. And, when he got to Jerusalem, he began to communicate to the people what he was about (v. 17-18).

In chapter three, Nehemiah set up divisions of labor and empowered the people to do their respective tasks. He did not lose sight of what needed to be accomplished so he scanned the environment for obstacles that would come from Israel's enemies. This is a key function of leadership—keeping watch over what's going on around you that could become a threat. This concept continues on into chapter four when the threat becomes even more ominous. We find more prayer and a plan to overcome any obstacles that did surface.

Chapter five gives another clear example for leadership—Nehemiah sets an unselfish example to the people. Verse 19 reveals more prayer, "Remember me, my God, for good, *according to* all that I have done for this people." We could discuss the merits of this prayer, whether it was vain, and so forth, but that's not the point—the point is how prayer is intermingled with the planning and leadership of Nehemiah's rebuilding project. In chapter six, more obstacles are overcome and then in chapter seven we find the project is completed. Was it easy? Definitely not, yet Nehemiah had a plan, he asked God to help him, he communicated to the persons who could supply the resources needed, he communicated to the people of Jerusalem, and he was vigilant in watching for and planning for obstacles that might arise. He prayed often. He was serving through leadership.

Chapter three of the book of Ezra also gives a good example of planning in the Old Testament. An altar was built and offerings were made. Supplies were obtained. Overseers were appointed, and the foundation was laid. The people then praised God. There are other Old Testament examples we could go into but you can do that at a later time as you're doing your own study around this topic. Always remember, whatever was written before time was for our learning (Romans 15:4).

Planning in today's congregation is necessary just as it has always been because of the myriad problems and issues that confront church leaders and congregations. The church has become institutionalized; different groups within a congregation may be making demands for change; the traditional views and values of the family has changed; there is generational and gender segmentation in the congregations; women's roles in the church are shifting, in many cases because of worldly pressures; and then there is the ever present dilemma of membership that does not get involved in the spiritual or physical work of the church.

Jesus gave his followers, the soon to be church, the following mission statement:

> "And Jesus came and spoke to them, saying, "All authority has been given to Me in heaven and on earth. Go therefore and make disciples of all the nations, baptizing them in the name of the Father and of the Son and of the Holy Spirit, teaching them to observe all things that I have commanded you; and lo, I am with you always, *even* to the end of the age." Amen. (Matthew 28:18-20)

How can we carry out Jesus' mission for the church if we do not plan? Planning is essential for any organization to do what it is intended to do and to accomplish the things it sets out to accomplish. This is where an understanding of the organization and organism are important. Each member of a congregation has a gift and without planning and knowing what those gifts are and taking advantage of them the congregation cannot reach its fullest potential to spread the gospel.

Jesus presents a clear reason for planning when he addressed the multitudes:

> For which of you, intending to build a tower, does not sit down first and count the cost, whether he has *enough* to finish *it*—lest, after he has laid the foundation, and is not able to finish, all who see *it* begin to mock him, saying, 'This man began to build and was not able to finish.' Or what king, going to make war against another king, does not sit down first and consider whether he is able with ten thousand to meet him who comes against him with twenty thousand? Or else, while the other is still a great way off, he sends a delegation and asks conditions of peace. So likewise, whoever of you does not forsake all that he has cannot be My disciple. (Luke 14:28-33)

Jesus was addressing those in the multitude who were considering becoming his disciples. He said, and I paraphrase, you cannot do it unless you first count the cost and that cost may be all that you have. Those folks in the crowd were the potential church that was still to come and Jesus was preparing them and essentially telling them to plan so they would know if they were capable of completing and living up to their decision to become his disciples and carry out his mission or direction for the church.

Congregations need workshops and lessons on congregational and leadership development. The purpose of these workshops and lessons should be to involve more of the members of the congregation as we come together and examine where we are as a congregation and where we want to be in the future. Planning helps an organization, in this case the church of the Lord, move from its present state to a future state by implementing a series of actions that will aid in the transition of moving from where it is to where it wants to be. If I read the Great Commission correctly, we are all to go and make disciples, we are all to baptize in the name of the Father and the Son and the Holy Spirit, and we are all to teach whoever we baptize to observe all things that Jesus has commanded us. Am I wrong in my understanding of this reading?

Warren Bennis, known for his expertise in leadership, was at one time the President of the University of Cincinnati. One time he was asked how he liked being the president of the university. He thought about it a few minutes and replied, "I don't know." Later, reflecting on the question, "he came to the realization that he loved being a college president but hated doing a college presidency" (as cited in Weick, 2001, p. 91).

He later resigned as university president because of this one rhetorical question and the subsequent reflection and went back to what he really liked, teaching and researching. This account of reflection made me wonder, how many of us love to BE Christians, we just don't like DOING Christianity? Is that a fair question? Does that make you think? I hope it does because it is not easy DOING Christianity. DOING Christianity takes a lot of time and effort and it takes good planning, both as an individual and as a congregation. Church planning is going to mean that we have to examine ourselves and decide whether we want to DO Christianity or not.

Jesus said,

> Therefore whoever hears these sayings of Mine, and does them, I will liken him to a wise man who built his house on the rock: and the rain descended, the floods came, and the winds blew and beat on that house; and it did not fall, for it was founded on the rock. "But everyone who hears these sayings of Mine, and does not do them, will be like a foolish man who built his house on the sand: and the rain descended, the floods came, and the winds blew

> and beat on that house; and it fell. And great was its fall. (Matt. 7:24-27)

Are we building our congregation on sand or are we taking the time to plan and pray about it and then take action to build the congregation on solid rock? That rock is our faith just as it was for the disciple Peter. I think many congregations are on a rock but I'm not sure about the thickness of the rock. To put a good congregational planning and leadership development process in place requires a lot of effort, a high level of commitment by both the congregational leaders and the members of the congregation, as well as much prayer by all parties involved. That will thicken the rock or foundation on which we are building!

Elders, deacons, and other ministry leaders should have a congregational planning and development process in place. How (the process) this is done is not important. The DOING is important. Simply stated, the process of planning should consist of information from the congregation's servant leaders in which they present the church's mission and their vision of how to get there. There should be continual prayer for the process and its success. The members should have an opportunity to give input to the congregational leaders and other members. The congregation has to be prepared for this planning by a series of lessons on what the Scriptures teach about planning, about the involvement of all members, and about how the mission of the congregation has to be linked to the Great Commission. It will not be easy in the beginning, but if the process is put in place and is consistently carried out over the years, the congregation and the church will benefit from it.

In Acts 15, we find that men from Judea were teaching that a man had to be circumcised before he could be saved. Paul and Barnabas, who were in Antioch on a mission trip, disagreed and disputed this teaching. The church then reached an agreement that Paul, Barnabas, and some others would take this issue to Jerusalem to the Apostles and elders there and present the question to them. We know from chapter 14 of Acts that it had already become the practice to appoint elders in the various congregations of the Lord's church.

In Jerusalem, they were received by the church and the apostles and elders (v. 4) and they reported the news of their activities and some of the Pharisees that had been saved also agreed that circumcision was necessary to be saved. See how big this problem is becoming! There was much discussion and Peter presented the position that this yoke should not be placed on the Gentiles. Then, Paul and Barnabas declared all of the good work that had been done with the Gentiles. James, the brother of Jesus, then presented more information based on the prophecies of the Old Testament and reminded the multitudes that were gathered that the Gentiles were to be called by the Lord (v. 17).

In verse 22 we find, "Then it pleased the apostles and elders, with the whole church, to send chosen men of their own company to Antioch with Paul and Barnabas, *namely,* Judas who was also named Barsabas, and Silas, leading men among the brethren." Several points here: 1) there was agreement among the apostles, the elders, and the whole church; 2) they sent men back to Antioch with the message of how the issue was settled; 3) some of those sent were "from their own company" so that the church in Antioch will receive the same answer from those they had sent as well as those "leading men" from Jerusalem; and 4) those "leading men" from the congregation that were sent, were not elders, not preachers, not deacons, but leading men in the congregation. This is indicative to me that there should be leaders in a congregation other than just the elders and deacons and preachers/ministers. I firmly believe the Scriptures teach us that all Christians should be leaders through their respective service and function in the body.

When they got back to Antioch, the letter or message was delivered to the multitude or church. The reason for going to this scriptural reference is to see that everyone was involved when there was an issue and I believe this same practice is necessary when congregations of the church of Christ begin a planning process. Modern day studies in the field of leadership suggest that when the leaders of an organization get the members of the organization involved in the planning strategy for the organization, they "buy in" to the process and are accepting of change that may have to occur to get from the present state of the organization to the future state of the organization that has been envisioned by the organization leaders.

There is not a specific reference that I can find in the New Testament that a planning process is necessary in a congregation, but the examples from the Old Testament coupled with the inferences that can be drawn from the New Testament presented here indicate that a planning process will help a congregation to grow, to solve problems, and to make decisions that everyone understands and that everyone has bought into and supports. The members of a congregation need planning in order to understand how their respective function "fits" into the mission.

I will leave you with this point from the Scriptures:

> "For which of you, intending to build a tower, does not sit down first and count the cost, whether he has *enough* to finish *it*—lest, after he has laid the foundation, and is not able to finish, all who see *it* begin to mock him, saying, 'This man began to build and was not able to finish.'" (Luke 14:28)

I pray that congregational leaders seriously consider putting a planning process in place if they do not already have one, and that that process will involve all the members of the congregation, if possible. If congregations already have a planning process in place, strengthen it by putting a strong development program in place for the members. For a planning process to work there must be communication between all members and the congregation's leadership, there must be prayers for its success, and there must be instruction for the congregation that demonstrates the support of the congregation's leaders.

If we look at the seven churches presented in chapters 2 and 3 of the Book of Revelation, of which church would you want to a member? If we, as a congregation, are going to be judged in those final days, how do you want to be described? I believe the Scriptures support a strong planning process in the church and I believe any congregation can rise to the process and that the church will be all the better for it.

References

Aristides (abt 125 AD). *The apology of Aristides the philosopher.* D.M. Kay, trans. (n.d). Retrieved 7/13/2008 from: http://www.earlychristianwritings.com/aristides.html.

Bennis, W. G. (1989). *On becoming a leader.* Reading, MA: Addison-Wesley Publishing Company.

Boles, H. L. (n.d.). *The Eldership of the Churches of Christ.* Nashville, TN: Gospel Advocate Company.

Bronowski, J. (n.d.).*The Common Sense of Science.* New York: Vintage Books.

Bruce, F.F. (1958). *The spreading flame: The rise and progress of Christianity from its first beginnings to the conversion of the English.* Grand Rapids, MI: Wm. B. Eerdmans Publishing Company.

Bruce, F. F. (1971). *New Testament History.* New York: Doubleday.

Brunner, E. (1953). *The misunderstanding of the church.* (H. Knight, translator). Philadelphia: The Westminster Press.

Clark, A. (n.d.). *Adam Clarke's Commentary on the New Testament.* Electronic Edition STEP Files Copyright © 1999, Parsons Technology, Inc., all rights reserved.

Cummings, T. G. & Worley, C. G. (2005). *Organization Development and Change.* Mason, Ohio: South-Western.

Denison, J.C., 2004, as cited in Holman Bible Dictionary, electronic version in QuickVerse, 2004, version 8.0.3.

Dubrin, A.J. (2007). *Leadership: Research findings, practice, and skills,* Boston: Houghton Mifflin Company.

Fair, I. A. (1996). *Leadership in the kingdom: Sensitive strategies for the church in a changing world.* Abilene, TX: ACU Press.

Ferguson, E. (1999), *Early Christians speak: Faith and life in the first three centuries* (3rd ed.). Abilene, TX: ACU Press.

Grimsley, R. W. (1964). *The church and its elders.* Abilene, TX: Quality Printing Company, Inc.

Hassell, C. B. (1886). *History of the church of God from the creation to A.D. 1885; Including especially the history of the Kehukee Primitive Baptist Association.* (Revised by Sylvester Hassell). Middleton, NY: Gilbert Beebe's Sons, Publishers.

Hughes, R. L., Ginnett, R. C., & Curphy, G. J. (2006). *Leadership: Enhancing the lessons of experience* (5th ed.). New York: McGraw-Hill/ Irwin.

Hunter, J.C. (2004). *The world's most powerful leadership principle: how to become a servant leader.* New York: Crown Publishing Group (Crown Business).

Knox, J. (1956). The ministry in the primitive church. In H.R. Niebuhr & D.D. Williams, (Eds.). *The ministry in historical perspectives (pp. 1-26).* San Francisco: Harper & Row Publishers.

Kouzes, J. M. & Posner, B. Z. (2002). *The leadership challenge* (3rd ed.). San Francisco: Jossey-Bass.

Leedy, P. D. & Ormrod, J. E. (2005). *Practical research: Planning and design* (8th ed.). Upper Saddle River, NJ: Pearson Prentice Hall.

Lenski, R.C.H. (1937). *St Paul's Epistles … I Timothy.* Minneapolis, MN: Augsburg Publishing House; cited in James Burton Commentaries, Vol. IX.

Lightfoot, J.B. (1898). The Christian Ministry, in *St Paul's epistle to the Philippians* (reprint). USA: Kessinger Publishing.

Lightfoot, N. R. (2003). *How we got the Bible* (3rd ed.). New York: MJF Books.

Lipscomb, D. *A commentary of the New Testament epistles.* Editor J.W. Shepherd. *I, II Thessalonians, I, II Timothy, Titus, and Philemon.*(vol. v). Nashville, TN: Gospel Advocate Company

Maxwell, J. C., & Parrott, L. (2005). *25 Ways to win with people: How to make others fell like a million bucks.* Nashville, TN: Thomas Nelson, Inc.

McDaniel, G. W. (1921). *The churches of the New Testament.* Nashville, TN: Broadman Press.

McGarvey, J.W. (1892). *New Commentary on Acts of Apostles.* Delight, AR: Gospel Light Publishing Company.

Moffatt, J. (1038). *The first five centuries of the church.* Nashville, TN: Cokesbury Press.

Richards, L.O. & Hoeldtke, C. (1980). *A theology of church leadership.* Grand Rapids, MI: Zondervan Publishing House. (p. 98).

Rogers, E. M. (1995). *Diffusion of innovations* (4th ed.). New York: The Free Press.

Rousseau, D. M. (1989). Psychological and implied contracts in organizations. *Employee Responsibilities and Rights Journal 2*(2), 121-139.

Schein, E. H. (1992). *Organization culture and leadership* (2nd ed). San Francisco: Jossey-Bass.

Survey finds major shifts in religions, (2008, February 28). *Atlanta Journal Constitution*, p. A3

The Barna Group (2007, December 3). *Barna finds four mega-themes in recent research.* Retrieved August 24, 2008 from www.barna.com.

United States Religious Demographic Profile (2006). Retrieved August 24, 2008 from pewforum.org.

Weick, K. E. (2001). Leadership as the legitimation of doubt. In W.G. Bennis, G.M Spreitzer, & T.G. Cummings (Eds.), *The future of leadership: Today's top leadership thinkers speak to tomorrow's leaders* (pp. 91-102). San Francisco: Jossey-Bass.

Yeakley, F. R., Jr. (1980). *Church leadership and organization.* Arvada, CO: Christian Communications, Inc.

Ziglar, Z. (2000). *See you at the top* (6th ed.). Gretna, LA: Pelican Publishing Company, Inc.

www.ingramcontent.com/pod-product-compliance
Ingram Content Group UK Ltd.
Pitfield, Milton Keynes, MK11 3LW, UK
UKHW041942190726
13854UKWH00004B/1743